PENGUIN BOOKS — GREAT IDEAS

The City of Ladies

Christine de Pizan
1364–1430

Christine de Pizan

The City of Ladies

TRANSLATED BY
ROSALIND BROWN-GRANT

PENGUIN BOOKS — GREAT IDEAS

PENGUIN BOOKS

Published by the Penguin Group
Penguin Group (USA) Inc., 375 Hudson Street, New York, New York 10014, U.S.A.
Penguin Group (Canada), 90 Eglinton Avenue East, Suite 700, Toronto,
Ontario, Canada M4P 2Y3 (a division of Pearson Penguin Canada Inc.)
Penguin Books Ltd, 80 Strand, London WC2R 0RL, England
Penguin Ireland, 25 St Stephen's Green, Dublin 2, Ireland (a division of Penguin Books Ltd)
Penguin Group (Australia), 250 Camberwell Road, Camberwell,
Victoria 3124, Australia (a division of Pearson Australia Group Pty Ltd)
Penguin Books India Pvt Ltd, 11 Community Centre, Panchsheel Park, New Delhi–110 017, India
Penguin Group (NZ), cnr Airborne and Rosedale Roads, Albany,
Auckland 1310, New Zealand (a division of Pearson New Zealand Ltd)
Penguin Books (South Africa) (Pty) Ltd, 24 Sturdee Avenue,
Rosebank, Johannesburg 2196, South Africa

Penguin Books Ltd, Registered Offices:
80 Strand, London WC2R 0RL, England

This edition published in Penguin Books (UK) 2005
Published in Penguin Books (USA) 2006

1 3 5 7 9 10 8 6 4 2

Translation copyright © Rosalind Brown-Grant, 1999
All rights reserved

Reprinted from *The Book of the City of Ladies*,
translated and introduced by Rosalind Brown-Grant (Penguin Classics, 1999).

ISBN 0 14 30.3754 4
CIP data available

Printed in the United States of America
Set in Monotype Dante

Contents

Part I

1. *Here begins the* Book of the City of Ladies, *the first chapter of which explains why and for what purpose the book was written*

One day, I was sitting in my study surrounded by many books of different kinds, for it has long been my habit to engage in the pursuit of knowledge. My mind had grown weary as I had spent the day struggling with the weighty tomes of various authors whom I had been studying for some time. I looked up from my book and decided that, for once, I would put aside these difficult texts and find instead something amusing and easy to read from the works of the poets. As I searched around for some little book, I happened to chance upon a work which did not belong to me but was amongst a pile of others that had been placed in my safe-keeping. I opened it up and saw from the title that it was by Matheolus. With a smile, I made my choice. Although I had never read it, I knew that, unlike many other works, this one was said to be written in praise of women. Yet I had scarcely begun to read it when my dear mother called me down to supper, for it was time to eat. I put the book to one side, resolving to go back to it the following day.

The next morning, seated once more in my study as is my usual custom, I remembered my previous desire to have a look at this book by Matheolus. I picked it up again and read on a little. But, seeing the kind of immoral language and ideas it contained, the content seemed to me likely to appeal only to those who enjoy reading works of slander and to be of no use whatsoever to anyone who wished to pursue virtue or to improve their moral standards. I therefore leafed through it, read the ending, and decided to switch to some more worthy and profitable work. Yet, having looked at this book, which I considered to be of no authority, an extraordinary thought became planted in my mind which made me wonder why on earth it was that so many men, both clerks and others, have said and continue to say and write such awful, damning things about women and their ways. I was at a loss as to how to explain it. It is not just a handful of writers who do this, nor only this Matheolus whose book is neither regarded as authoritative nor intended to be taken seriously. It is all manner of philosophers, poets and orators too numerous to mention, who all seem to speak with one voice and are unanimous in their view that female nature is wholly given up to vice.

As I mulled these ideas over in my mind again and again, I began to examine myself and my own behaviour as an example of womankind. In order to judge in all fairness and without prejudice whether what so many famous men have said about us is true, I also thought about other women I know, the many princesses and countless ladies of all different social ranks who have shared their private and personal thoughts with me. No matter which way I looked at it and no matter how much I turned the question over in my mind, I could find no evidence from my own experience to bear out such a negative view of female nature and habits. Even so, given that I could scarcely find a moral work by any author which didn't devote some chapter or paragraph to attacking the female sex, I had to accept their unfavourable opinion of women since it was unlikely that so many learned men, who seemed to be endowed with such great intelligence and insight into all things, could possibly have lied on so many different occasions. It was on the basis of this one simple argument that I was forced to conclude that, although my understanding was too crude and ill-informed to recognize the great flaws in myself and other women, these men had to be in the right. Thus I preferred to give more weight to what others said than to trust my own judgement and experience.

I dwelt on these thoughts at such length that it was as if I had sunk into a deep trance. My mind became flooded with an endless stream of names as I recalled all the authors who had written on this subject. I came to the conclusion that God had surely created a vile thing when He created woman. Indeed, I was astounded that such a fine craftsman could have wished to make such an appalling object which, as these writers would have it, is like a vessel in which all the sin and evil of the world has been collected and preserved. This thought inspired such a great sense of disgust and sadness in me that I began to despise myself and the whole of my sex as an aberration in nature.

With a deep sigh, I called out to God: 'Oh Lord, how

can this be? Unless I commit an error of faith, I cannot doubt that you, in your infinite wisdom and perfect goodness, could make anything that wasn't good. Didn't you yourself create woman especially and then endow her with all the qualities that you wished her to have? How could you possibly have made a mistake in anything? Yet here stand women not simply accused, but already judged, sentenced and condemned! I just cannot understand this contradiction. If it is true, dear Lord God, that women are guilty of such horrors as so many men seem to say, and as you yourself have said that the testimony of two or more witnesses is conclusive, how can I doubt their word? Oh God; why wasn't I born a male so that my every desire would be to serve you, to do right in all things, and to be as perfect a creature as man claims to be? Since you chose not to show such grace to me, please pardon and forgive me, dear Lord, if I fail to serve you as well as I should, for the servant who receives fewer rewards from his lord is less obligated to him in his service.'

Sick at heart, in my lament to God I uttered these and many other foolish words since I thought myself very unfortunate that He had given me a female form.

2. Christine tells how three ladies appeared to her, and how the first of them spoke to her and comforted her in her distress

Sunk in these unhappy thoughts, my head bowed as if in shame and my eyes full of tears, I sat slumped against the arm of my chair with my cheek resting on my hand. All of a sudden, I saw a beam of light, like the rays of the sun, shine down into my lap. Since it was too dark at that time of day for the sun to come into my study, I woke with a start as if from a deep sleep. I looked up to see where the light had come from and all at once saw before me three ladies, crowned and of majestic appearance, whose faces shone with a brightness that lit up me and everything else in the place. As you can imagine, I was full of amazement that they had managed to enter a room whose doors and windows were all closed. Terrified at the thought that it might be some kind of apparition come to tempt me, I quickly made the sign of the cross on my forehead.

With a smile on her face, the lady who stood at the front of the three addressed me first: 'My dear daughter, don't be afraid, for we have not come to do you any harm, but rather, out of pity on your distress, we are here to comfort you. Our aim is to help you get rid of those misconceptions which have clouded your mind and made you reject what you know and believe in fact to be the truth just because so many other people have come out with the opposite opinion. You're acting like that fool in the joke who falls asleep in the mill and whose friends play a trick on him by dressing him up in women's clothing. When he wakes up, they manage to convince him that he is a woman despite all evidence to the contrary! My dear girl, what has happened to your sense? Have you forgotten that it is in the furnace that gold is refined, increasing in value the more it is beaten and fashioned into different shapes? Don't you know that it's the very finest things which are the subject of the most intense discussion? Now, if you turn your mind to the very highest realm of all, the realm of abstract ideas, think for a moment whether or not those philosophers whose views against women you've been citing have ever been proven wrong. In fact, they are all constantly correcting each other's opinions, as you yourself should know from reading Aristotle's *Metaphysics* where he discusses and refutes both their views and those of Plato and other philosophers. Don't forget the Doctors of the Church either, and Saint Augustine in particular, who all took issue with Aristotle himself on certain matters, even though he is considered to be the greatest of all authorities on both moral and natural philosophy. You seem to have accepted the philosophers' views as articles of faith and thus as irrefutable on every point.

'As for the poets you mention, you must realize that they sometimes wrote in the manner of fables which you have to take as saying the opposite of what they appear to say. You should therefore read such texts according to the grammatical rule of *antiphrasis*, which consists of interpreting something that is negative in a positive light, or vice versa. My advice to you is to read those passages where they criticize women in this way and to turn them to your advantage, no matter what the author's original intention was. It could be that Matheolus is also meant to be read like this because there are some passages in his book which, if taken literally, are just out-and-out heresy. As for what these authors – not just Matheolus but also the more authoritative writer of the *Romance of the Rose* – say about the

God-given, holy state of matrimony, experience should tell you that they are completely wrong when they say that marriage is insufferable thanks to women. What husband ever gave his wife the power over him to utter the kind of insults and obscenities which these authors claim that women do? Believe me, despite what you've read in books, you've never actually *seen* such a thing because it's all a pack of outrageous lies. My dear friend, I have to say that it is your naivety which has led you to take what they come out with as the truth. Return to your senses and stop worrying your head about such foolishness. Let me tell you that those who speak ill of women do more harm to themselves than they do to the women they actually slander.'

[. . .]

8. Christine explains how Reason instructed her and helped her to begin digging up the ground in order to lay the foundations

Lady Reason replied to my words, saying: 'Stand up now, daughter, and without further delay let us make our way to the Field of Letters. There we will build the City of Ladies on flat, fertile ground, where fruits of all kinds flourish and fresh streams flow, a place where every good thing grows in abundance. Take the spade of your intelligence and dig deep to make a great trench all around where you see the line I have traced I'll help to carry away the hods of earth on my shoulders.'

Obeying her instructions, I jumped to my feet: thanks to the three ladies, my body felt much stronger and lighter than before. She took the lead and I followed on behind. When we came to the spot she had described, I began to excavate and dig out the earth with the spade of my intelligence, just as she had directed me to do. The first fruit of my labours was this: 'My lady, I'm remembering that image of gold being refined in the furnace that you used before to symbolize the way many male writers have launched a full-scale attack on the ways of women. I take this image to mean that the more women are criticized, the more it redounds to their glory. But please tell me exactly what it is that makes so many different authors slander women in their writings because, if I understand you correctly, they are wrong to do so. Is it Nature that makes them do this? Or, if it is out of hatred, how can you explain it?'

Reason answered my questions, saying: 'My dear daughter, in order to help you see more clearly how things stand, let me carry away this first load of earth. I can tell you that, far from making them slander women, Nature does the complete opposite. There is no stronger or closer bond in the world than that which Nature, in accordance with God's wishes, creates between man and woman. Rather, there are many other different reasons which explain why men have attacked women in the past and continue to do so, including those authors whose works you have already mentioned. Some of those who criticized women did so with good intentions: they wanted to rescue men who had already fallen into the clutches of depraved and corrupt women or to prevent others from suffering the same fate, and to encourage men generally to avoid leading a lustful and sinful existence. They therefore attacked all women in order to persuade men to regard the entire sex as an abomination.'

'My lady,' I said, 'forgive me for interrupting you. Were they right to do so, since they were acting with good intentions? Isn't it true that one's actions are judged by one's intentions?'

'You're wrong, my dear girl,' she replied, 'because there is no excuse for plain ignorance. If I killed you with good intentions and out of stupidity, would I be in the right? Those who have acted in this way, whoever they may be, have abused their power. Attacking one party in the belief that you are benefiting a third party is unfair. So is criticizing the nature of all women, which is completely unjustified, as I will prove to you by analogy. Condemning all women in order to help some misguided men get over their foolish behaviour is tantamount to denouncing fire, which is a vital and beneficial element, just because some people are burnt by it, or to cursing water just because some people are drowned in it. You could apply the same reasoning to all manner of things which can be put to either good or bad use. In none of these cases should you blame the thing in itself if foolish people use it unwisely. You yourself have made these points elsewhere in your writings. Those who subscribe to these opinions, whether in good or bad faith, have overstepped the mark in order to make their point. It's like somebody cutting up the whole piece of cloth in order to make himself a huge coat simply because it's not going to cost him anything and no one is going to object. It thus stops anyone else from using the material. If instead, as you yourself have rightly remarked, these writers had tried to find ways to save men from indulging in vice and from frequenting debauched women by attacking only the morals and the habits of those who were evidently guilty of such behaviour, I freely admit that they would have produced texts which were extremely useful. It's true that there's nothing worse than a woman who is dissolute and depraved: she's like a monster, a creature going against its own nature, which is to be timid, meek and pure. I can assure you that those writers who condemn the entire female sex for being sinful, when in fact there are so many women who are extremely virtuous, are not acting with my approval. They've committed a grave error, as do all those who subscribe to their views. So let us throw out these horrible, ugly, misshapen stones from your work as they have no place in your beautiful city.

'Other men have criticized women for different reasons: some because they are themselves steeped in sin, some because of a bodily impediment, some out of sheer envy, and some quite simply because they naturally take delight in slandering others. There are also some who do so because they like to flaunt their erudition: they have come across these views in books and so like to quote the authors whom they have read.

'Those who criticize the female sex because they are inherently sinful are men who have wasted their youth on dissolute behaviour and who have had affairs with many different women. These men have therefore acquired cunning through their many experiences and have grown old without repenting of their sins. Indeed, they look back with nostalgia on the appalling way they used to carry on when they were younger. Now that old age has finally caught up with them and the spirit is still willing but the flesh has grown weak, they are full of regret when they see that, for them, the "good old days" are over and they can merely watch as younger men take over from where they have had to leave off. The only way they can release their frustration is to attack women and to try to stop others from enjoying the pleasures that they themselves used to take. You very often see old men such as these going around saying vile and disgusting things, as in the case of your Matheolus, who freely admits that he is just an impotent old man who would still like to satisfy his desires. He's an excellent example to illustrate my point as he's typical of many other similar cases.

'Yet, thank goodness, not all old men are full of depravity and rotten to the core like a leper. There are many other fine, decent ones whose wisdom and virtue have been nourished by me and whose words reflect their good character, since they speak in an honourable and sober fashion. Such men detest all kinds of wrongdoing and slander. Thus, rather than attacking and defaming individual sinners, male or female, they condemn all sins in general. Their advice to others is to avoid vice, pursue virtue and stick to the straight and narrow.

'Those men who have attacked women because of their own bodily impediments, such as impotence or a deformed limb, are all bitter and twisted in the mind. The only pleasure they have to compensate for their incapacity is to slander the female sex since it is women who bring such joy to other men. That way they are convinced that they can put others off enjoying what they themselves have never had.

'Those men who have slandered the opposite sex out of envy have usually known women who were cleverer and more virtuous than they are. Out of bitterness and spite, envious men such as these are driven to attack all women, thinking that they can thereby undermine these individuals' good reputation and excellent character, as in the case of the author of *On Philosophy* whose name I've forgotten. In this book, he goes to great lengths to argue that men should on no account praise women and that those who do so are betraying the title of his book: their doctrine is no longer "philosophy" but "philofolly". However, I can assure you that it is definitely he who is the arch-exponent of "philofolly" because of all the false reasoning and erroneous conclusions he comes out with in his book.

'As for those men who are slanderous by nature, it's not surprising if they criticize women, given that they attack everyone indiscriminately. You can take it from me that any man who wilfully slanders the female sex does so because he has an evil mind, since he's going against both reason and nature. Against reason, because he is lacking in gratitude and failing to acknowledge all the good and indispensable things that woman has done for him both in the past and still today, much more than he can ever repay her for. Against nature, in that even the birds and the beasts naturally love their mate, the female of the species. So man acts in a most unnatural way when he, a rational being, fails to love woman.

'Finally, there are those who dabble in literature and delight in mimicking even the very finest works written by authors who are greatly superior to them. They think themselves to be beyond reproach since they are merely repeating what others have already said. Believe me, this is how they set about making their defamatory remarks. Some of them scribble down any old nonsense, verse without rhyme or reason, in which they discuss the ways of women, or princes, or whoever it might be, when it is they themselves, whose habits leave much to be desired, who are most in need of moral self-improvement. Yet the common folk, who are as ignorant as they are, think that it's the best thing they've ever read.'

9. How Christine dug over the earth: in other words, the questions which she put to Reason and the answers she received from her

'Now that I have prepared and set out this great task for you, you should carry on the task of digging up the ground, following the line which I have laid down.'

In obedience to Reason's wishes, I set to with all my might, saying, 'My lady, why is it that Ovid, who is considered to be the greatest of poets (though others, myself included, think that Virgil is more worthy of that accolade, if you don't mind my saying so), made so many derogatory remarks about women in his writings, such as the *Art of Love*, the *Remedies of Love* and other works?'

Reason replied: 'Ovid was a man very well versed in the theory and practice of writing poetry and his fine mind allowed him to excel in everything he wrote. However, his body was given over to all kinds of worldliness and vices of the flesh: he had affairs with many women, since he had no sense of moderation and showed no loyalty to any particular one. Throughout his youth, he behaved like this only to end up with the reward he richly deserved: he lost not just his good name and his possessions, but even some parts of his body! Because he was so licentious, both in the way he carried on and in the encouragement he gave to others to do the same, he was finally sent into exile. Even when he was brought back from banishment by some of his followers, who were influential young men of Rome, he couldn't help himself from falling into exactly the same pattern as before. So finally he was castrated and deprived of his organs because of his immorality. He's another good example of what I was telling you about just now: once he realized that he could no longer indulge in the same kind of pleasures as before, he began to attack women with his sly remarks in an attempt to make others despise them too.'

'My lady, your words certainly ring true. However, I've seen another book by an Italian writer called Cecco d'Ascoli who, if I remember correctly, comes from the Marches or Tuscany. In this work, he says some extraordinarily unpleasant things which are worse than anything else I've ever read and which shouldn't be repeated by anybody with any sense.'

Reason's response was: 'My dear girl, don't be surprised if Cecco d'Ascoli slandered the whole of womankind since he hated and despised them all. Being unspeakably wicked, he tried to make all other men share his nasty opinion about women. He too got what he deserved: thanks to his heretical views, he suffered a shameful death at the stake.'

'My lady, I've also come across another little book in Latin, called *On the Secrets of Women*, which states that the female body is inherently flawed and defective in many of its functions.'

Reason replied, 'You shouldn't need any other evidence than that of your own body to realize that this book is a complete fabrication and stuffed with lies. Though some may attribute the book to Aristotle, it is unthinkable that a philosopher as great as he would have produced such outrageous nonsense. Any woman who reads it can see that, since certain things it says are the complete opposite of her own experience, she can safely assume that the rest of the book is equally unreliable. Incidentally, do you remember the part at the beginning where he claims that one of the popes excommunicated any man found either reading the book out loud to a woman or giving it to her to read for herself?'

'Yes, my lady, I do remember that passage.'

'Do you know what evil motive drove him to put such vile words at the front of his book for gullible, foolish men to read?'

'No, my lady, you'll have to tell me.'

'It was because he didn't want women to get hold of his book and read it or have someone else read it to them for fear that if they did, they would pour scorn on it and would recognize it for the utter rubbish that it is. By this ruse, he thought he could trick the men who wanted to read his text.'

'My lady, amongst the other things he said, I seem to remember that, after going on at great length about female children being the result of some weakness or deficiency in the mother's womb, he claimed that Nature herself is ashamed when she sees that she has created such an imperfect being.'

'Well, my dear Christine, surely it's obvious that those who come out with this opinion are totally misguided and irrational? How can Nature, who is God's hand-maiden, be more powerful than her own master from whom she derives her authority in the first place? It is God almighty who, at the very core of His being, nurtured the idea of creating man and woman. When He put His divine wish into action and made Adam from the clay of the fields of Damascus, He took him to dwell in the earthly paradise, which has always been the noblest place on this lowly earth. There He put Adam to sleep and created the body of woman from one of his ribs. This was a sign that she was meant to be his companion standing at his side, whom he would love as if they were one flesh, and not his servant lying at his feet. If the Divine Craftsman Himself wasn't ashamed to create the female form, why should Nature be? It really is the height of stupidity to claim otherwise. Moreover, how was she created? I'm not sure if you realize this, but it was in God's image. How can anybody dare to speak ill of something which bears such a noble imprint? There are, however, some who are foolish enough to maintain that when God made man in His image, this means His physical body. Yet this is not the case, for at that time God had not yet adopted a human form, so it has to be understood to mean the soul, which is immaterial intellect and which will resemble God until the end of time. He endowed both male and female with this soul, which He made equally noble and virtuous in the two sexes. Whilst we're still on the subject of how the human body was formed, woman was created by the very finest of craftsmen. And where exactly was she made? Why, in the earthly paradise. What from? Was it from coarse matter? No, it was from the finest material that had yet been invented by God: from the body of man himself.'

'My lady, from what you've told me, I can see that woman is a very noble creature. Yet, all the same, wasn't it Cicero who said that man should not be subject to woman and that he who did so abased himself because it is wrong to be subject to one who is your inferior?'

Reason answered, 'It is he or she who is the more virtuous who is the superior being: human superiority or inferiority is not determined by sexual difference but by the degree to which one has perfected one's nature and morals. Thus, happy is he who serves the Virgin Mary, for she is exalted even above the angels.'

'My lady, it was one of the Catos, the one who was a great orator, who declared that if woman hadn't been created, man would converse with the gods.'

Reason's reply was: 'Now you see an example of someone who was supposed to be very wise coming out with something very foolish. It is because of woman that man sits side by side with God. As for those who state that it is thanks to a woman, the lady Eve, that man was expelled from paradise, my answer to them would be that man has gained far more through Mary than he ever lost through Eve. Humankind has now become one with God, which never would have happened if Eve hadn't sinned. Both men and women should praise this fault of Eve's since it is because of her that such an honour has been bestowed on them. If human nature is fallen, due to the actions of one of God's creatures, it has been redeemed by the Creator Himself. As for conversing with the gods if womankind hadn't been invented, as this Cato claims; his words were truer than he knew. Being a pagan, he and those of his faith believed that both heaven and hell were ruled by the gods. But the ones in hell are what we call devils. So it's definitely true to say that men would be conversing with the gods of hell if Mary had not come into the world!'

[. . .]

11. *Christine asks Reason why women aren't allowed in courts of law, and Reason's reply*

'Most honourable and worthy lady, your excellent arguments have satisfied my curiosity in so many areas. Yet, if you don't mind, I'd like you to explain to me why women are allowed neither to present a case at a trial, nor bear witness, nor pass sentence since some men have claimed that it's all because of some woman or other who behaved badly in a court of law.'

'My dear daughter, that whole ridiculous story is a malicious fabrication. However, if you wanted to know the causes and reasons behind everything, you would never get to the end of it. Even Aristotle, though he explained many things in his *Problemata* and *Categories*, was not equal to the task. But, dear Christine, to come back to your question, you might as well ask why God didn't command men to perform women's tasks and women those of men. In answer, one could say that just as a wise and prudent lord organizes his household into different domains and operates a strict division of labour amongst his workforce, so God created man and woman to serve Him in different ways and to help and comfort one another, according to a similar division of labour. To this end, He endowed each sex with the qualities and attributes which they need to perform the tasks for which they are cut out, even though sometimes humankind fails to respect these distinctions. God gave men strong, powerful bodies to stride about and to speak boldly, which explains why it is men who learn the law and maintain the rule of justice. In those instances where someone refuses to uphold the law which has been established by right, men must enforce it through the use of arms and physical strength, which women clearly could not do. Even though God has often endowed many women with great intelligence, it would not be right for them to abandon their customary modesty and to go about bringing cases before a court, as there are already enough men to do so. Why send three men to carry a burden which two can manage quite comfortably?

'However, if there are those who maintain that women aren't *intelligent* enough to learn the law, I would contradict them by citing numerous examples of women of both the past and the present who were great philosophers and who excelled in many disciplines which are much more difficult than simply learning the laws and the statutes of men. I'll tell you more about these women in a moment. Moreover, in reply to those who think that women are lacking in the ability to govern wisely or to establish good customs, I'll give you examples from history of several worthy ladies who mastered these arts. To give you a better idea of what I'm saying, I'll even cite you a few women from your own time who were widowed and whose competence in organizing and managing their households after their husbands' deaths attests to the fact that an intelligent woman can succeed in any domain.'

12. About the Empress Nicaula

'Tell me, if you can, whether you have ever read about a king who was more skilled in politics, statesmanship and justice and who maintained a more magnificent court than the great Empress Nicaula? The many different vast and extensive lands which she held under her dominion were ruled by the famous kings known as pharaohs, from whom she herself was descended. However, it was this lady who first established laws and good customs in her realm, thus putting end once and for all to the primitive ways of the people in the countries under her control, even to the savage habits of the bestial Ethiopians. Those authors who have written about Nicaula praise her in particular for the way in which she brought civilization to her subjects. She was the heir of the pharaohs, inheriting a huge territory which included the kingdoms of Arabia, Ethiopia, Egypt and the island of Meroë, a long, broad stretch of land, which was extremely fertile, located in the middle of the Nile. She governed all of her territory with exemplary skill. What more can I tell you about this lady? Nicaula was so wise and so powerful that even the Holy Scriptures speak of her great abilities. She herself established just laws by which to rule her people. In nobility and wealth, she surpassed almost any man who ever lived. She was extremely well versed in both the arts and the sciences and was so proud that she never condescended to take a husband nor wanted any man to be at her side.'

[. . .]

14. More discussion and debate between Christine and Reason

'My lady, you have truly spoken well, and your words are like music to my ears. Yet, despite what we've said about intelligence, it's undeniable that women are by nature fearful creatures, having weak, frail bodies and lacking in physical strength. Men have therefore argued that it is these things that make the female sex inferior and of lesser value. To their minds, if a person's body is defective in some way, this undermines and diminishes that person's moral qualities and thus it follows that he or she is less worthy of praise.'

Reason's reply was, 'My dear daughter, this is a false conclusion which is completely untenable. It is definitely the case that when Nature fails to make a body which is as perfect as others she has created, be it in shape or beauty, or in some strength or power of limb, she very often compensates for it by giving that body some greater quality than the one she has taken away. Here's an example: it's often said that the great philosopher Aristotle was very ugly, with one eye lower than the other and a deformed face. Yet, if he was physically misshapen, Nature certainly made up for it by endowing him with extraordinary intellectual powers, as is attested by his own writings. Having this extra intelligence was worth far more to him than having a body as beautiful as that of Absalom.

'The same can be said of the emperor Alexander the Great, who was extremely short, ugly and sickly, and yet, as is well known, he had tremendous courage in his soul. This is also true of many others. Believe me, my dear friend, it doesn't necessarily follow that a fine, strong body makes for a brave and courageous heart. Courage comes from a natural, vital force which is a gift from God that He allows Nature to implant in some rational beings more than in others. This force resides in the mind and the heart, not in the bodily strength of one's limbs. You very often see men who are well built and strong yet pathetic and cowardly, but others who are small and physically weak yet brave and tough. This applies equally to other moral qualities. As far as bravery and physical strength are concerned, neither God nor Nature has done the female sex a disservice by depriving it of these attributes. Rather, women are lucky to be deficient in this respect because they are at least spared from committing and being punished for the acts of appalling cruelty, the murders and terrible violent deeds which men who are equipped with the necessary strength have performed in the past and still do today. It probably would have been better for such men if their souls *had* spent their pilgrimage through this mortal life inside the weak body of a woman. To return to what I was saying, I am convinced that if Nature decided not to endow women with a powerful physique, she none the less made up for it by giving them a most virtuous disposition: that of loving God and being fearful of disobeying His commandments. Women who don't act like this are going against their own nature.

'However, dear Christine, you should note that God clearly wished to prove to men that, just because *all* women are not as physically strong and courageous as men generally are, this does not mean that the entire female sex is lacking in such qualities. There are in fact several women who have displayed the necessary courage, strength and bravery to undertake and accomplish extraordinary deeds which match those achieved by the great conquerors and knights mentioned in books. I'll shortly give you an example of such a woman.

'My dear daughter and beloved friend, I've now prepared a trench for you which is good and wide, and have
emptied it of earth which I have carried away in great
loads on my shoulders. It's now time for you to place
inside the trench some heavy, solid stones which will
form the foundations of the walls for the City of Ladies.
So take the trowel of your pen and get ready to set to
with vigour on the building work. Here is a good, strong
stone which I want you to lay as the first of your city's
foundations. Don't you know that Nature herself used
astrological signs to predict that it should be placed here
in this work? Step back a little now and let me put it into
position for you.'

[. . .]

16. About the Amazons

'There is a country near the land of Europe which lies
on the Ocean, that great sea that covers the whole world.
This place is called Scythia, or the land of the Scythians.
It once happened that, in the course of a war, all the
noblest male inhabitants of this country were killed.
When their womenfolk saw that they had lost all their
husbands, brothers and male relatives, and that only very
young boys and old men were left, they took courage
and called together a great council of women, resolving
that, henceforth, they would lead the country themselves, free from male control. They issued an edict
which forbade any man from entering their territory,

but decided that, in order to ensure the survival of their race, they would go into neighbouring countries at certain times of the year and return thereafter to their own land. If they gave birth to male children, they would send them away to be with their fathers, but the female children they would bring up themselves. In order to uphold this law, they chose two of the highest-born ladies to be queens, one of whom was called Lampheto and the other Marpasia. No sooner was this done than they expelled all the men who were left in the country. Next, they took up arms, women and girls together, and waged war on their enemies, laying waste to their lands with fire and sword and crushing all opposition until none remained. In short, they wreaked full revenge for their husbands' deaths.

'This is how the women of Scythia began to bear arms. They were later known as the Amazons, a name which means "they who have had a breast removed". It was their custom that, by a technique known only to this race of women, the most noble of them would have the left breast burnt off at a very early age in order to free them up to carry a shield. Those young girls who were of non-noble birth would lose the right breast so that they could more easily handle a bow. They took such pleasure in the pursuit of arms that they greatly expanded their territory by the use of force, thus spreading their fame far and wide. To get back to what I was saying, the two queens Lampheto and Marpasia each led a great army into various countries and were so successful that they conquered a large part of Europe and the region of Asia, subjugating many kingdoms to their rule.

They founded many towns and cities including the Asian city of Ephesus, which has long been justly renowned. Of these two queens, it was Marpasia who died first in battle and who was replaced by a young daughter of hers, a beautiful and noble maiden called Synoppe. This girl was so proud that she chose never to sleep with a man, preferring instead to remain a virgin until her death. Her only love and sole pleasure in life was the pursuit of arms: she never tired of going into battle and seizing new lands. She also avenged her mother's death fully by putting to the sword the entire enemy population and laying waste to their whole country, adding it to the others which she went on to conquer.'

[. . .]

27. Christine asks Reason if God has ever blessed a woman's mind with knowledge of the highest branches of learning, and Reason's reply

Having listened to what Reason said, I answered, 'My lady, God truly performed wonders by endowing these women you've just been telling me about with such extraordinary powers. But, if you don't mind, please tell me if, amongst all the other favours He has shown to women, God ever chose to honour any of them with great intelligence and knowledge. Do they indeed have an aptitude for learning? I'd really like to know why it is that men claim women to be so slow-witted.'

Reason's reply was: 'Christine, from what I've already

told you, it should be obvious that the opposite of what they say is true. To make the point more clearly for you, I'll give you some conclusive examples. I repeat – and don't doubt my word – that if it were the custom to send little girls to school and to teach them all sorts of different subjects there, as one does with little boys, they would grasp and learn the difficulties of all the arts and sciences just as easily as the boys do. Indeed, this is often the case because, as I mentioned to you before, although women may have weaker and less agile bodies than men, which prevents them from doing certain tasks, their minds are in fact sharper and more receptive when they do apply themselves.'

'My lady, what are you saying? If you please, I'd be grateful if you would expand on this point. No man would ever accept this argument if it couldn't be proved, because they would say that men generally know so much more than women.'

She replied, 'Do you know why it is that women know less than men?'

'No, my lady, you'll have to enlighten me.'

'It's because they are less exposed to a wide variety of experiences since they have to stay at home all day to look after the household. There's nothing like a whole range of different experiences and activities for expanding the mind of any rational creature.'

'So, my lady, if they have able minds which can learn and absorb as much as those of men, why don't they therefore know more?'

'The answer, my dear girl, is that it's not necessary for the public good for women to go around doing what men are supposed to do, as I informed you earlier. It's quite adequate that they perform the tasks for which they are fitted. As for this idea that experience tells us that women's intelligence is inferior to that of men simply because we see that those around us generally know less than men do, let's take the example of male peasants living in remote countryside or high mountains. You could give me plenty of names of places where the men are so backward that they seem no better than beasts. Yet, there's no doubt that Nature made them as perfect in mind and body as the cleverest and most learned men to be found in towns and cities. All this comes down to their lack of education, though don't forget what I said before about some men and women being more naturally endowed with intelligence than others. I'll now go on to prove to you that the female sex is just as clever as the male sex, by giving you some examples of women who had fine minds and were extremely erudite.'

28. Reason begins to speak about ladies who were blessed with great learning, starting with the noble maiden Cornificia

'The parents of the noble maiden Cornificia used a clever trick to send her to school along with her brother Cornificius when they were both young children. This little girl applied her extraordinary intelligence so well to her studies that she began to take a real delight in learning. It would have been extremely difficult to stifle this talent in her, for she refused all normal female occupations in order to devote herself to her books. After much dedication, she soon became an excellent and learned poet not solely in the field of poetry itself but also in philosophy, which she just drank in as if it were mother's milk. She was so motivated to excel in all the different disciplines that she soon outshone her brother himself no mean poet, in all branches of scholarship.

'Moreover, she was not content simply to study the theoretical side of learning but wished to put her own knowledge into practice. Taking up her pen, she composed several distinguished works which, at the time of Saint Gregory, were held in great esteem, as he himself indicates in his writings. The great Italian author Boccaccio says of Cornificia in his book: "What a great honour it is for a woman to put aside all feminine things and to devote her mind to studying the works of the greatest scholars." He confirms what I've been telling you when he goes on to say that those women who have no confidence in their own intellectual abilities act as if they were born in the backwoods and had no concept of what is right and moral, letting themselves be discouraged and saying that they're fit for nothing but fussing over men and bearing and bringing up children. God has given every woman a good brain which she could put to good use, if she so chose, in all the domains in which the most learned and renowned men excel. If women wished to study, they are no more excluded from doing so than men are; and could easily put in the necessary effort to acquire a good name for themselves just as the most distinguished of men delight in doing. My dear daughter, see how Boccaccio himself echoes what I've been saying and note how much he approves of learning in a woman and praises them for it.'

[. . .]

30. About Sappho, who was an extremely fine poet and philosopher

'No less learned than Proba was Sappho, a maiden from the city of Mytilene. This Sappho was physically very beautiful, and also charming in her speech, manner and bearing. However, the finest of her attributes was her superb intellect, for she was a great expert in many different arts and sciences. Moreover, she was not only familiar with the writings and treatises of others but was herself an author who composed many new works. The poet Boccaccio pays tribute to her, describing her in these delightful terms: "Sappho, spurred on by her fine mind and burning desire, devoted herself to her studies and rose above the common, ignorant herd, making her home on the heights of Mount Parnassus; in other words, at the summit of knowledge itself. Through her extra-ordinary boldness and daring, she won the good will of the Muses; that is, she immersed herself in the arts and sciences. She thus made her way through the lush forest full of laurels, may trees, delicious-scented flowers of different hues and sweet-smelling herbs which is the place where Grammar, Logic, Geometry, Arithmetic, and noble Rhetoric dwell. She travelled down this path until she eventually came to the deep cave of Apollo, god of knowledge, where she found the bubbling waters of the spring of Castalia. There she took up a plectrum and played lovely tunes on the harp with the nymphs leading the dance; that is to say, she learnt the art of musical chords as well as the rules of harmonics."

'This description of Sappho by Boccaccio should be understood to refer to the depth of her learning and to the great erudition of her works which, as the Ancients themselves pointed out, are so complex that even the most intelligent and educated men have difficulty in grasping their meaning. Her books, which are exquisitely written and still popular today, offer an excellent model for those of later generations who want to perfect the art of writing verse. She invented many new forms of song and poetry, including lays, sorrowful complaints, strange love laments and other poems inspired by different emotions which are beautifully wrought and are now called Sapphic poems in her honour. On the subject of this lady's works, Horace recalls that a book of her verse was found under the pillow of the great philosopher Plato, Aristotle's teacher, when he died.

'To cut a long story short, Sappho was so famous for her learning that her native city decided to dedicate a prominent bronze statue to her in order to honour her and record her achievements for posterity. She earned herself a place amongst the greatest poets whose glory, according to Boccaccio, far outshines the mitres of bishops, the coronets and crowns of kings and even the palm wreaths and laurel garlands of those who are victorious in battle. I could give you many more examples of brilliant women, such as the Greek woman Leontium, an excellent philosopher, who dared to put forward clearly reasoned arguments against Theophrastus, a thinker who was highly regarded in his own time.'

[. . .]

33. Christine asks Reason if any woman has ever invented new forms of knowledge

I, Christine, on hearing Reason's words, took up this matter and said to her, 'My lady, I can clearly see that you are able to cite an endless number of women who were highly skilled in the arts and sciences. However, I'd like to ask you if you know of any woman who was ingenious, or creative, or clever enough to invent any new useful and important branches of knowledge which did not previously exist. It's surely less difficult to learn and follow a subject which has already been invented than it is to discover something new and unknown by oneself.'

Reason replied, 'Believe me, many crucial and worthy arts and sciences have been discovered thanks to the ingenuity and cleverness of women, both in the theoretical sciences which are expressed through the written word, and in the technical crafts which take the form of manual tasks and trades. I'll now give you a whole set of examples.

'First of all, I'll tell you about the noble Nicostrata, whom the Italians called Carmentis. This lady was the daughter of the king of Arcadia whose name was Pallas. She was extraordinarily intelligent and endowed by God with special intellectual gifts, having such a vast knowledge of Greek literature and being able to write so wisely, elegantly and with such eloquence that the poets of the time claimed in their verse that she was loved by the god Mercury. They similarly thought that her son, who was in his day equally renowned for his intelligence, was the offspring of this god, rather than of her husband. Because of various upheavals that occurred in her native land, Nicostrata, accompanied by her son and a whole host of other people who wanted to go with her, set off for Italy in a large fleet of ships and sailed up the River Tiber. It was here that she went ashore and climbed up a great hill which she named Mount Palatine after her father. On this hill, where the city of Rome was subsequently founded, she, her son and her followers built themselves a castle. As she found the indigenous population to be very primitive, she laid down a set of rules for them to observe and encouraged them to live a rational and just existence. Thus it was she who first established laws in this country that was to become so famous for developing a legal system from which all known laws would be derived.

'Amongst all the other attributes that this lady possessed, Nicostrata was particularly blessed with the gift of divine inspiration and prophecy. She was thus able to predict that her adopted country would one day rise above all others to become the most magnificent and glorious realm on earth. To her mind, therefore, it would not be fitting for this country which would outshine and conquer the rest of the world to use an inferior and crude set of alphabetical letters which had originated in a foreign country. Moreover, Nicostrata wished to transmit her own wisdom and learning to future generations in a suitable form. She therefore set her mind to inventing a new set of letters which were completely different from those used in other nations. What she created was the ABC – the Latin alphabet – as well as the rules for constructing words, the distinction between vowels and consonants and the bases of the science of grammar. She gave this knowledge and this alphabet to the people, in the hope that they would become universally known. It was truly no small or insignificant branch of knowledge that this lady invented, nor should she receive only paltry thanks for it. This ingenious science proved so useful and brought so much good into the world that one can honestly say that no nobler discovery was ever made.

'The Italians were not lacking in gratitude for this great gift, and rightly so, since they heralded it as such a marvellous invention that they venerated her more highly than any man, worshipping Nicostrata/Carmentis like a goddess in her own lifetime. When she died, they built a temple dedicated to her memory, situated at the foot of the hill where she had made her home. In order to preserve her fame for posterity, they borrowed various terms from the science she had invented and even used her own name to designate certain objects. In honour of the science of Latin that she had invented, the people of the country called themselves Latins. Furthermore, because *ita* in Latin is the most important affirmative term in that language, being the equivalent of *oui* in French, they did not stop at calling their own realm the land of the Latins, but went so far as to use the name Italy to refer to the whole country beyond their immediate borders, which is a vast area comprising many different regions and kingdoms. From this lady's name, Carmentis, they also derived the Latin word *carmen*, meaning "song". Even the Romans, who came a long time after her, called one of the gates of the city the *Porta Carmentalis*. These names have not been changed since and are still the same today, no matter how the fortunes of the Romans have fared or which mighty emperor was in power.

'My dear Christine, what more could you ask for? Could any mortal man be said to have done anything so splendid? But don't think that she's the only example of a woman who invented many new branches of learning . . .'

34. About Minerva, who invented countless sciences, including the art of making arms from iron and steel

'Minerva, as you yourself have noted elsewhere, was a maiden from Greece who was also known as Pallas. This girl was so supremely intelligent that her contemporaries foolishly declared her to be a goddess come down from the heavens, since they had no idea who her parents were and she performed deeds that had never been done before. As Boccaccio himself points out, the fact that they knew so little about her origins meant that they were all the more astonished at her great wisdom, which surpassed that of every other woman of her time. She employed her skilfulness and her immense ingenuity not just in one domain but in many. First of all, she used her brilliance to invent various Greek letters called characters which can be used to write down a maximum number of ideas in a minimum number of words. This wonderfully clever invention is still used by the Greeks today. She also invented numbers and developed ways of using them to count and perform quick calculations. In short, she was so ingenious that she created many arts and techniques that had not previously been discovered, including the art of making wool and cloth. It was she who first had the idea of shearing sheep and developing the whole process of untangling, combing and carding the wool with various instruments, cleaning it, breaking down the fibres on metal spikes and spinning it on the distaff, whilst also inventing the tools needed for weaving it into cloth and making it into fine fabric.

'Likewise, she discovered how to make oil from pressing olives and how to extract the juice from other sorts of fruit.

'Likewise, she invented the art of building carts and chariots in order to carry things more easily from one place to another.

'Likewise, an invention of this lady's which was all the more marvellous for being such an unlikely thing for a woman to think of, was the art of forging armour for knights to protect themselves in battle and weapons of iron and steel for them to fight with. She taught this art first to the people of Athens, whom she also instructed in how to organize themselves into armies and battalions and to fight in serried ranks.

'Likewise, she invented flutes, pipes, trumpets and other wind instruments.

'This lady was not only extraordinarily intelligent but also supremely chaste, remaining a virgin all her life. It was because of her exemplary chastity that the poets claimed in their fables that she struggled long and hard with Vulcan, the god of fire, but finally overcame and defeated him. This story can be interpreted to mean that she conquered the passions and desires of the flesh which so vigorously assail the body when one is young. The Athenians held this girl in the highest esteem, worshipping her as if she were a deity and calling her the goddess of arms and warfare because she was the first to invent these arts. She was also known as the goddess of wisdom, thanks to her great intelligence.

'After her death, the people of Athens built a temple dedicated to her, in which they placed a statue representing wisdom and warfare in the likeness of a girl. This statue had terrible fierce eyes to symbolize both the duty of a knight to enforce justice and the inscrutability of the thoughts of a wise man. The statue had a helmet on its head, to suggest the idea that a knight must be hardened in battle and have unfailing courage, and that the plans of a wise man should be shrouded in secrecy. It was also dressed in chainmail, to represent the power of the estate of knighthood as well as the foresight of a wise man who arms himself against the vicissitudes of Fortune. The statue held a great spear or lance as an emblem of the fact that a knight must be the rod of justice and that a wise man launches his attacks from a safe distance. Round the statue's neck hung a shield or buckler of crystal, meaning that a knight must always be vigilant and ready to defend the country and the people and that a wise man has a clear understanding of all things. In the centre of this shield was the image of the head of a serpent known as a Gorgon, to suggest the idea that a knight must be cunning and stalk his enemies like a snake whilst a wise man must be wary of all the harm that others might do to him. To guard the statue, they placed next to it a night bird – an owl – to signify that a knight must be prepared, if needs be, to protect the country both day and night, and that a wise man must be alert at all times to do what is right. This lady Minerva was greatly revered for a long time and her fame spread to many other countries, where they also dedicated temples to her. Even centuries later, when the Romans were at the height of their powers, they incorporated her image into their pantheon of gods.'

35. About Queen Ceres, who invented agriculture and many other arts

'Ceres was queen of the Sicilians in very ancient times. Thanks to her great ingenuity, it was she who was responsible for inventing both the science and the techniques of agriculture as well as all the necessary tools. She taught her subjects how to round up and tame their cattle and train them to take the yoke. Ceres also invented the plough, showing her people how to use the blade to dig and slice through the soil, and all the other skills needed for this task. Next she taught them how to scatter the seed on the ground and to cover it over. Once the seed had taken root and grown into shoots, she revealed to them how to cut the sheaves and thresh them with a flail in order to separate the wheat from the chaff. Ceres then demonstrated to them how to grind the grain between heavy stones and to construct mills, going on to show them how to prepare flour and make it into bread. Thus this lady encouraged men who had been living like beasts off acorns, wild grasses, apples and holly berries to eat a more noble diet.

'Ceres didn't stop there: she gathered together her people, who at that time were used to wandering about like animals making their temporary homes in woods or moorlands, into large groups and taught them how to build proper towns and cities and to live in communities. She thereby brought humankind out of its primitive state and introduced it to a more civilized and rational way of life. The poets wrote a fable about Ceres which tells how her daughter was abducted by Pluto, god of the underworld. Because of her great knowledge and all the good that she had brought into the world, the people of the time venerated her, calling her the goddess of corn.'

36. About Isis, who discovered the art of making gardens and growing plants

'Thanks to her extensive knowledge of horticulture, Isis was not only queen of Egypt but also the highly revered goddess of the Egyptians. The fables tell how Isis was loved by Jupiter, who turned her into a cow and then back into her original form, all of which is an allegory of her great learning, as you yourself have pointed out in your *Letter of Othea to Hector*. For the benefit of the Egyptians, she also invented certain types of characters to represent their language which could be used to write down ideas in a concise way.

'Isis was the daughter of Inachos, king of the Greeks, and sister of Phoroneus, who was a very wise man. It so happened that this lady and her brother left Greece for Egypt and it was there that she showed the people many different things, including how to create gardens, grow plants and graft cuttings of one species on to another. She also set up a number of fine and decent laws which she encouraged the Egyptians to live by, since up until then they had been in a very primitive state without a properly established system of justice. In short, Isis did so much for them that they honoured her with great ceremony both in her own lifetime and after her death. Her fame spread throughout the world, with temples and oratories consecrated to her springing up all over. Even when Rome was at its peak, the Romans erected a temple in her honour where they performed great sacrifices and solemn rites observing the same customs which the Egyptians used to worship her.

'This noble lady's husband was named Apis, whom the pagans mistakenly believed to be the son of the god Jupiter and of Niobe, daughter of Phoroneus. The ancient historians and poets make great mention of this man.'

[. . .]

43. Christine asks Reason if women are naturally endowed with good judgement, and Reason replies to her question

I, Christine, came back to Reason, saying: 'My lady, it is now clear to me that God has truly made women's minds sharp enough to learn, understand and retain any form of knowledge. Praise be to Him for this! However, I'm always surprised at how many people you see whose minds are very quick to pick up and grasp all that they are shown and who are mentally agile and clever enough to master any discipline they please, attaining great learning through their dedication to their studies, but yet seem to lack judgement when it comes to their personal morals and public behaviour. This is true even of some of the most famous and erudite scholars. There's no doubt that knowledge of the sciences should help inculcate moral values. So, if you please, my lady, I'd be keen to know whether women's minds, which both you and my own experience have proved to me to be capable of understanding the most complex matters in sciences and other disciplines, are just as proficient at learning the lessons which good judgement teaches us. In other words, can women distinguish between what is the right and the wrong thing to do? Can they modify their current behaviour on the basis of past experience? Can they use the example of the present to anticipate how they should conduct themselves in the future? In my view, this is what good judgement consists of.'

Reason replied: 'You're quite right, my dear girl. Yet don't forget that this faculty that you're talking about is inherent in both men and women, and that some are more generously endowed with it than others. Note too that good judgement does not come from learning, though learning can help perfect it in those who are naturally that way inclined, since, as you know, two forces moving in the same direction are stronger and more powerful than a single force moving on its own. Therefore, in my opinion, anyone who has naturally good judgement or good sense and who also manages to attain learning is thoroughly deserving of praise. But, as you yourself have pointed out, some have one but not the other: one is a gift from God and is an innate quality, whereas the other is only acquired after much study. Both, however, are good.

'There are those who would maintain that it is better to have good judgement and no learning than to have great learning but bad judgement. This is a highly contro-versial proposition that raises all sorts of questions. You could say that the best person is the one who contributes most to the common good. In that case, it's undeniable that learned individuals help others most by sharing their knowledge with them, no matter how much good judgement they might possess. This is because individuals' faculty of judgement only lasts as long as their lifetime: when they die, it does, too. On the other hand, learning which has been acquired endures for ever, in that the good reputation of those who possess it never dies and they can teach their knowledge to others as well as pass it on in books for future generations to discover. Their learning does not therefore die with them, as I can prove to you by the example of Aristotle and all the others who first brought the sciences into the world. This type of acquired knowledge has been more beneficial to humankind than all the good judgement shown by those figures of the past who had no learning, even though many of them used their good sense to govern and administer their empires and kingdoms most wisely. The fact is, these deeds are transient and vanish with time, whereas learning is indestructible.

'However, I'm going to set these matters aside for others to resolve since they are not strictly relevant to our task of building the city. Instead, let's go back to what you originally asked me about whether women naturally have good judgement. On this question, I can give you a firm "yes". You should be able to gather this not just from what I've already told you but also from observing the way in which women generally go about doing their traditionally female duties. If you care to look closely, you'll discover that for the most part women prove themselves to be extremely attentive, diligent and meticulous in running a household and seeing to everything as best they can. Sometimes, those women who have lazy husbands annoy them by giving the impression that they are nagging them, telling them what to do and trying to be the voice of authority in the house; though husbands like this are just putting a bad slant on what most wives do with all good intentions. The next part of what I have to say will be largely derived from the "Epistle of Solomon" which talks about good wives such as these.'

44. The 'Epistle of Solomon' from the Book of Proverbs

'Whoever finds a valiant woman, one of sound judgement, will be a husband who lacks for nothing. Her fame spreads far and wide and her husband puts his faith in her for she brings him nothing but good and prosperity at all times. She looks for and acquires wool, in other words she sets her maid servants a worthy task to keep them gainfully employed and her household well stocked, and she herself lends a hand. She is like the ship of a merchant which brings all good things to shore and provides the bread. She rewards those who deserve it and they are her intimate friends. In her house, there is plenty to eat, even for the servants. She weighs up the price of a piece of land before buying it and she uses her good sense to plant the vines which will keep the household in wine. Full of courage and resolve, she girds her loins with strength and toughens up her arms with continuous hard work. Even in the dark of night, the light of her labours still shines through. She toils at the heavy tasks yet doesn't neglect women's work either, for she does her fair share. She extends a helping hand to the poor and brings them comfort in their suffering. By her efforts, the house is protected against the cold and the snow and her servants' clothing is lined. She dresses herself in silk and purple: that is, in integrity and splendour. Her husband too cuts an honourable figure when he is seated in the top ranks with the most venerable people in the land. She makes fine linen cloth, which she sells, and wraps herself in strength and glory. For this, she will have everlasting joy. Words of wisdom spring from her lips and her tongue is ruled by gentleness. She makes sure that the household is fully provided for and does not eat the bread of idleness. Her children's behaviour shows that she is their mother and their actions reveal her tender care. Her husband's fine appearance does her credit. She governs her daughters in all matters, even when they are fully grown. She despises the trappings of glory and the transience of beauty. Such a woman will fear the Lord and be praised, and He will reward her for her labours as they attest to her virtue far and wide.'

[. . .]

48. About Lavinia, daughter of King Latinus

'Lavinia, queen of the Laurentines, was similarly renowned for her good sense. Descended from the same Cretan king, Saturn, whom I've just mentioned, she was the daughter of King Latinus. She later wed Aeneas, although before her marriage she had been promised to Turnus, king of the Rutulians. Her father, who had been informed by an oracle that she should be given to a Trojan prince, kept putting off the wedding despite the fact that his wife, the queen, was very keen for it to take place. When Aeneas arrived in Italy, he requested King Latinus's permission to enter his territory. He was not only granted leave to do so but was immediately given Lavinia's hand in marriage. It was for this reason that Turnus declared war on Aeneas, a war which caused many deaths and in which Turnus himself was killed. Having secured the victory, Aeneas took Lavinia as his wife. She later bore him a son, even though he himself died whilst she was still pregnant. As her time grew near, she became very afraid that a man called Ascanius, Aeneas's elder son by another woman, would attempt to murder her child and usurp the throne. She therefore went off to give birth in the woods and named the newborn baby Julius Silvius. Vowing never to marry again, Lavinia conducted herself with exemplary good judgement in her widowhood and managed to keep the kingdom intact, thanks to her astuteness. She was able to win her stepson's affection and thus defuse any animosity on his part towards her or his stepbrother. Indeed, once he had finished building the city of Alba, Ascanius left to make his home there. Meanwhile, Lavinia ruled the country with supreme skill until her son came of age. This child's descendants were Romulus and Remus, who later founded the city of Rome. They in turn were the ancestors of all the noble princes who came after them.

'What more can I tell you, my dear Christine? It seems to me that I've cited sufficient evidence to make my point, having given enough examples and proofs to convince you that God has never criticized the female sex more than the male sex. My case is conclusive, as you have seen, and my two sisters here will go on to confirm this for you in their presentation of the facts. I think that I have fulfilled my task of constructing the enclosure walls of the City of Ladies, since they're all now ready and done. Let me give way to my two sisters: with their help and advice you'll soon complete the building work that remains.'

End of the First Part of the Book *of the City of Ladies.*

Part II

1. The first chapter tells of the ten Sibyls

After the first lady, whose name was Reason, had finished speaking, the second lady, called Rectitude, turned to me and said, 'My dear Christine, I mustn't hang back from performing my duty: together we must construct the houses and buildings inside the walls of the City of Ladies which my sister Reason has now put up. Take your tools and come with me. Don't hesitate to mix the mortar well in your inkpot and set to on the masonry work with great strokes of your pen. I'll keep you well supplied with materials. With the grace of God, we'll soon have put up the royal palaces and noble mansions for the glorious and illustrious ladies who will come to live in this city for evermore.'

On hearing this honourable lady's words, I, Christine, replied to her, saying, 'Most excellent lady, here I stand ready before you. I will obey your every command, for my only wish is to do your bidding.'

She then answered me, 'My dear friend, look at these beautiful gleaming stones, more precious than any others in the world, that I have quarried and cut ready for you to use in the building work. Have I stood idly by whilst you were toiling away so hard with Reason? You must now arrange them in the order that I shall give you, following the line that I have traced for you.

'Amongst the highest rank of ladies of great renown are the wise sibyls who were extraordinarily knowledgeable. According to the most authoritative sources, there were ten sibyls, though some maintain there were only nine. My dear Christine, take good note of all this: what greater gift of divine revelation did God ever bestow on any prophet, even the most beloved, than that which He granted to these noble ladies I'm talking about? Didn't He confer on them the holy spirit of prophecy which allowed them to speak and write so straightforwardly and clearly that it was as if they were recounting past and completed actions in the manner of a chronicle, rather than anticipating events that would happen in the future? They even spoke more plainly and in greater detail than any prophet about the coming of Christ, which happened a long time after their day. These ladies kept their virginity intact and their bodies unsullied for the whole of their lives. All ten of them were called Sibyl, but this shouldn't be taken to be a proper name. The word "sibyl" in fact means "one who is privy to the thoughts of God". They were all given this name because their prophecies were of such momentous events that they could only have known of them if they had had access to the mind of God Himself. It's therefore a title of office rather than the name of an individual. Though they were all born in different countries of the world and lived in different eras, they all foresaw great future events including, with particular clarity, the birth of

Christ, as I've already mentioned. Moreover, all ten of them were pagans, not even of the Jewish faith.

'The first sibyl came from the land of Persia, and for this reason is called Persica. The second one was from Libya, hence she was known as Libica. The third, born in the temple of Apollo at Delphi, was therefore called Delphica. It was she who predicted the destruction of Troy long before it occurred and she to whom Ovid dedicated a few lines in one of his books. The fourth one was from Italy: her name was Cimeria. The fifth, born in Babylon, was called Herophile: she was the one who prophesied to the Greeks who had come to consult her that they would destroy both Troy and its citadel, Ilium, and that Homer would give an untruthful version of these events in his writings. She was also known as Erythrea, for that was the name of the island where she made her home and where her books were subsequently discovered. The sixth one came from the island of Samos, and was called Samia. The seventh was known as Cumana, because she was born in the Italian city of Cumae, in the region of Campania. The eighth was named Hellespontina, for she came from Hellespont on the plains of Troy: she flourished during the time of Cyrus and the famous author Solon. The ninth one, called Phrygica, was from Phrygia, and she not only spoke at length about the fall of many different kingdoms but also described in vivid detail the coming of the false prophet Antichrist. The tenth was called Tiburtina, also known as Albunea, whose writings are held in great esteem because she wrote about Jesus Christ most clearly. Despite the fact that these sibyls were all of pagan origin, each of them eventually repudiated this faith on the grounds that it was wrong to worship a multiplicity of gods, that there was only one true God, and that all idols were false.'

[. . .]

5. About Cassandra and Queen Basine, as well as more about Nicostrata

'That Nicostrata whom we discussed earlier was also a prophetess. As soon as she crossed the River Tiber and had climbed up on to Mount Palatine with her son Evander, of whom the history books make great mention, she prophesied that on that hill would be built the most famous city that had ever existed, one which would rule over all other earthly kingdoms. In order to be the first person to lay down a founding stone, she constructed a fortress there, as we have said before, and it was on this spot that Rome was founded and subsequently built.

'Likewise, wasn't the noble Trojan maiden Cassandra, daughter of King Priam of Troy and sister of the illustrious Hector, also a prophetess, she who was so learned that she knew all the arts? Having chosen never to take any man for her lord, no matter how high-born a prince he might be, this girl foresaw what would happen to the Trojans and was forever sunk in sorrow. The more she saw the glory of Troy flourish and prosper in the period before the conflict between the Trojans and the Greeks began, the more she wept, wailed and lamented. The sight of the city in all its wealth and magnificence, and of her brothers in all their splendour, especially the noble Hector who was so full of valour, made it impossible for Cassandra to keep to herself all the horror that was to come. On seeing the war break out, her grief intensified and she never left off crying, shrieking and imploring her father and brothers to make peace with the Greeks for heaven's sake, warning them that otherwise the war would destroy every one of them. But her words were all in vain for no one believed her. Moreover, since she refused to be silent but understandably gave full vent to her sorrow at all this destruction and killing, she was often beaten by her father and brothers who told her that she was mad. Yet she never let up for a moment: even if her life depended on it, she would never stop telling them about what was going to happen. In the end, in order to have some peace and to block out the incessant noise she made, they had to shut her up in a distant room far away from other people. However, it would have been better for them if they had believed her, because everything came to pass just as she had said. They eventually regretted what they had done, but by then it was too late.

'Likewise, weren't the prophecies of Queen Basine equally extraordinary, she who had been married to the king of Thuringia and then became the wife of Childeric, the fourth king of France, as the chronicles recall? The story goes that, on her wedding night, she persuaded King Childeric that if he kept himself chaste that night he would receive a marvellous vision. Thereupon she told him to get up and go to the bedroom window and to describe what he could see outside. The king did as she said and it seemed to him that he could see great beasts such as unicorns, leopards and lions coming and going in the palace. Turning round to the queen in terror, he asked her what it all meant. She replied that she would reveal the answer to him in the morning and reassured him that he had nothing to fear but should go back to the window again. This he did, and the second time he thought he saw fierce bears and enormous wolves which seemed to be attacking each other. The queen sent him back to the window a third time and he thought he could see dogs and other small creatures tearing each other to pieces. The king was so horrified and amazed at these things that the queen had to explain to him that the animals he had seen in his vision represented their descendants, the successive generations of French princes who would one day sit on the throne. The different types of animal symbolized what the temperament and behaviour of these various princes would be like.

'So, you can clearly see, my dear Christine, how often God has disclosed His secrets to the world through women.'

[. . .]

7. *Christine addresses Lady Rectitude*

'My lady, the more evidence I see and hear which proves that women are innocent of everything that they have been accused of, the more obvious it is to me how in the wrong their accusers are. Yet I can't help myself from mentioning a custom which is quite common amongst men and even some women, which is that when wives are pregnant and give birth to a daughter, their husbands are very often unhappy and disgruntled that they didn't bear them a son. Their silly wives, who should be over-joyed that God has delivered them safely and should thank Him with all their hearts, are also upset because they see that their husbands are distressed. But why is it, my lady, that they are so displeased? Is it because girls are more trouble than boys or less loving and caring towards their parents than male children are?'

Rectitude replied, 'My dear friend, since you've asked me why this happens, I can assure you that those who upset themselves tend to do so out of ignorance and stupidity. However, the main reason why they are unhappy is because they worry how much it's going to cost them to marry off their daughters since they will have to pay for it out of their own pockets. Others, though, are dismayed because they're afraid of the danger that a young and innocent girl can be led astray by the wrong sort of people. Yet neither of these reasons stands up to scrutiny. As for being worried that their daughters will disgrace themselves, all the parents have to do is bring them up properly when they're little, with the mother setting them an example through her own respectable behaviour and good advice; though if the mother has lax morals, she will hardly be a fit example for the daughter to follow. Daughters should be kept on a tight rein away from bad company and taught to fear their parents because bringing infants and children up strictly helps to establish good conduct later in life. Likewise, on the question of the expense involved, I would say that if the parents, whatever social class they may be, looked carefully at what it costs them to set their sons up or to pay for them to study or learn a trade, let alone all the extra money which their sons spend on disreputable acquaintances and unnecessary luxuries, they would soon realize that sons are scarcely less of a financial burden than daughters. Not to mention all the terrible anguish and worry that many sons frequently inflict on their parents by getting into nasty fights and vicious brawls or by falling into depraved habits, all this to the shame of their parents and at their expense. To my mind, this far outweighs any distress that their daughters might cause them.

'See how many names you can cite of sons who actually looked after their aged parents with kindness and consideration, as they should do. Though one can find both past and present examples, they're rather thin on the ground and their assistance comes only at the last minute. What usually happens is that, when they're all grown up, having been treated like a god by their parents and having learnt a trade or studied thanks to their father's help, or become rich and affluent by some stroke of good fortune, if their father falls on hard times or into destitution, they'll turn their backs on him and be ashamed and embarrassed when they see him. If, on the other hand, the father is well off, they can't wait for him to die so that they can get their hands on his estate. God knows how many sons of great lords and wealthy men long for the death of their parents in order to inherit their lands and possessions. Petrarch definitely spoke the truth when he said: "O foolish man, you wish to have children but you can have no deadlier enemies than these. If you are poor, they will despise you and will pray for your death so as to be rid of you. If you are rich, they will pray for it all the more in order to grab your wealth." I don't mean to say that all sons are like this, but many of them are. Moreover, if they're married, God knows how insatiable they can be as they suck their mother and father dry to the extent that they wouldn't care if the poor old things starved to death as long as they can inherit the lot. What dreadful offspring! If their mothers are widowed, instead of comforting them and being a rod and staff to them in their old age, they pay them back terribly for all the love and devotion their mothers have spent on bringing them up. Bad children have the idea that everything should belong to them, so if their mothers don't give them all they want, they don't hesitate to pour down their curses upon them. Heaven knows what kind of respect this is to show one's mother! Worse still, some of them think nothing of taking their mothers to court and bringing a case against them. That's the reward that many parents get for having spent their whole lives putting their money to one side for the benefit of their children. Plenty of sons are like this, and it may be too that some daughters are of the same ilk. But if you look closely, I think you'll find that there are more unworthy sons than daughters.

'Even if all male children *were* dutiful, the fact remains that you see more daughters than sons keeping their mothers and fathers company. They not only visit them more often, but also comfort them and look after them more when they're old and infirm. The reason for this is that boys tend to go out and about in the world whereas girls tend to be retiring and stay closer to home, as you yourself can attest. Though your brothers are very loving and devoted sons, they have gone out into the world whilst you have stayed behind alone to take care of your dear mother and are the main comfort to her in her old age. To sum up, I would say that those who are upset and unhappy at having daughters are completely deluded. Whilst we're on this subject, I'd like to tell you about several women mentioned amongst others in the history books who were very kind and caring towards their parents.'

8. *Here begins a series of daughters who loved their parents, the first of whom is Drypetina*

'Drypetina, Queen of Laodicea, was very loving to-wards her father. She was the daughter of the great King Mithradates and was so devoted to him that she followed him into all his battles. This girl was extremely ugly, for she had two sets of teeth, a very severe deformity. However, she loved her father so much that she never left his side, in good times or in bad. Despite the fact that she was the queen and lady of a vast realm, which meant that she could have lived a safe and comfortable life in her own country, she preferred to share her father's sufferings and hardships whenever he went off to war. Even when he was defeated by the mighty Pompey, she still did not abandon him but looked after him with great care and dedication.'

[. . .]

12. Here Rectitude explains that the houses of the city have been completed and that it is time they were filled with inhabitants

'My dearest friend, it seems to me that our building is well underway and that the City of Ladies now has plentiful housing all along its wide streets. The royal palaces are completed and the defence towers and keeps are now standing proud, tall enough to be seen from miles away. It's high time that we began to fill this city with people. It should not stand deserted or empty but should be full of illustrious ladies, as they alone are welcome here. How happy the inhabitants of our city will be! They will have no cause to fear being thrown out of their homes by enemy hordes, for this place has a special property which means that those who move into it will never be dispossessed. A new Realm of Femininia is at hand, except that this one is so much more perfect than the previous one because the ladies who live here will have no need to leave their territory in order to breed the new generations of women who will inherit their realm down the ages. The ladies we're going to invite here will be sufficient in number to last for all time.

'Once we have filled the city with worthy citizens, my sister, Lady Justice, will come bringing with her the queen, a magnificent lady who surpasses all others, accompanied by a host of the noblest princesses. It is they who will occupy the finest buildings and will make their homes in the lofty towers. So it's all the more urgent that, when the queen comes, she should find the city full of excellent ladies ready to receive her with all honours as their supreme mistress and as the empress of their sex. What type of citizens shall we bring? Will they be dissolute women of ill repute? Most certainly not! They will all be valiant ladies of great renown, for we could wish for no worthier population nor more beautiful adornment to our city than such virtuous and honourable women as these. Come now, Christine, let's set out in search of our ladies.'

13. Christine asks Lady Rectitude if it's true what men and books say about the institution of marriage being unbearable because women are so impossible to live with. In her reply, Rectitude begins by discussing the great love that women have for their husbands

Whilst we were doing as Rectitude had said and were on our way to fetch the ladies we were looking for, I said to her as we walked along, 'My lady, you and Reason have conclusively replied to all the questions and queries that I was unable to answer for myself and I think that I'm now much better informed than I was before on these matters. Thanks to you two, I have discovered that women are more than capable of undertaking any task which requires physical strength or of learning any discipline which requires discernment and intelligence. However, I would now like to ask your opinion about something which is weighing very heavily on my mind. Is it true what so many men say and so many authors in their books claim about it being the fault of women and their shrewish, vengeful nagging that the married state is such a constant hell for men? There are plenty of people who maintain that this is the case, arguing that women care so little for their husbands and their company that there is nothing which irritates them more. In order to avoid this misery and these problems, many authors have advised men to be wise and not to marry at all, on the grounds that there are no women – or hardly any – who are faithful to their spouses. This view is even echoed in the *Letter of Valerius to Ruffinus* which quotes Theophrastus who, in his book, stated that no wise man would take a wife because women cause trouble, lack affection, and gossip incessantly. He also says that if a man gets married thinking that he'll be well looked after and well cared for if he falls ill, he'd be much better off being attended by a loyal servant, who would also cost him a lot less too. If the wife falls ill, on the other hand, he'll be all anxious and will feel obliged not to leave her side. Theophrastus came out with much more in this vein, but I won't go into it any further. My dear lady, if such things are true, it would seem that these faults are so awful that they cancel out completely whatever good qualities or virtues a woman might have.'

Rectitude replied, 'My dear Christine, as you yourself said earlier on this subject, it's certainly easy to win your case when there's no one to argue against you. But believe me when I tell you that the books which put forward these ideas were definitely not written by women. Indeed, I have no doubt that if one wanted to write a new book on the question of marriage by gathering information based on the facts; one would come up with a very different set of views. My dear friend, as you yourself know, there are so many wives who lead a wretched existence bound in marriage to a brutish husband who makes them suffer greater penance than if they were enslaved by Saracens. Oh God, how many fine and decent women have been viciously beaten for no good reason, heaped with insults, obscenities and curses, and subjected to all manner of burdens and indignities, without uttering even a murmur of protest. Not to mention all those wives who are laden down with lots of tiny mouths to feed and lie starving to death in penury whilst their husbands are either out visiting places of depravity or living it up in town or in taverns. All that wives such as these get for supper when their husbands come home is a good hiding. I ask you, am I telling lies? Haven't you ever seen any of your neighbours being treated in this way?'

I replied, 'Yes, my lady. I've seen many women treated like this and I felt sorry for them.'

'I can well believe it. As for those husbands who are anxious when their wives fall ill, I ask you, my dear friend, do you know of any? Without going into further detail, let me tell you that all this rubbish that has ever been said and written about wives is just a string of falsehoods tied together. It is the husband who is the master of the wife, and not the other way round. A man would never allow himself to be dominated by a woman. However, let me assure you that not all marriages are like this. There are some married couples who love each other, are faithful to each other, and live together in peace: in these cases it is both spouses who are sensible, kind and gentle. Though there are bad husbands, there are also some who are decent, honourable and wise. The women who have the good fortune to marry them should thank God for giving them so much happiness here on this earth. You yourself can attest to this since you couldn't have wished for a better husband than you had. In your opinion, he surpassed all other men in kindness, gentleness, loyalty and affection, and you will never stop grieving for his death in your heart. Whilst it's undeniable that there are many fine women who are badly treated by their contrary husbands, it's also true to say that some wives *are* wilful and unreasonable. Indeed, if I claimed that all wives were paragons of virtue, I would quite rightly be accused of being a liar. However, these women are in the minority. Anyway, I'd rather not discuss such women because they're like creatures who go totally against their nature.

'Talking about good wives instead, let's go back to what that Theophrastus, whom you mentioned earlier, said about a sick man being as well looked after and as faithfully attended by a servant as by a wife. You see countless good and loyal wives who serve their husbands in sickness or in health with as much loving care as if they were gods! I don't think you're going to find many servants like that. Since we're on this subject, I'll now give you some examples of wives who adored their husbands and were utterly devoted to them. Now, thank the Lord, we can come back to our city with a fine host of decent and respectable ladies whom we can invite inside. Here is the noble Queen Hypsicratea, who was once wife of the mighty King Mithradates. Because she belongs to such ancient times and is of such inestimable worth, she shall be the first to take her place in the magnificent palace which has been prepared for her.'

14. About Queen Hypsicratea

'How could anyone show more love for another person than the beautiful Hypsicratea did for her husband, she who was so kind and loyal? This lady was the wife of the great King Mithradates who ruled over lands where twenty-four different languages were spoken. Despite the fact that this king was the most powerful on earth, the Romans waged a terrible war on him. In all the time that he was engaged in his lengthy and arduous battles, his good wife never left him, no matter where he went. As was the barbarian custom, this king also had several concubines. However, this noble lady bore her husband such a deep love that she refused to let him go anywhere without her and frequently went off with him into battle. Though the fate of the kingdom was at stake and the threat of death at the hands of the Romans ever present, she travelled everywhere with him to far-off places and strange lands, crossing seas and perilous deserts and never once failing to be his faithful companion at his side. Her affection for him was so strong that she deemed that no man could possibly serve her lord with such perfect loyalty as she could.

'So, contrary to what the philosopher Theophrastus says on the subject, this lady was well aware that kings and princes can often have disloyal servants who serve them badly. Therefore, like the faithful lady she was, she devoted herself to ensuring that her lord's every possible need was met. Though she had to endure many hardships, she followed him through thick and thin. Since it was impractical for her to wear women's clothing in these conditions, and it was thought improper that the wife of such a great king and warrior should be seen at his side in battle, she cut off her finest womanly attribute, her long, golden hair, in order to disguise herself as a man. Neither did she give a thought to protecting her complexion, for she strapped on a helmet and her face soon grew dirty from all the sweat and dust. Her lovely, graceful body she clad in armour and weighed down with a coat of chainmail. She took off all her precious rings and costly jewellery and instead roughened her hands from carrying heavy axes and spears, as well as a bow and arrows. Round her waist she wore no elegant girdle but a sword. Because of the great love and loyalty she bore her husband, this lady so thoroughly adapted herself to her new surroundings that her charming and delicate young body, which was made for softer and more pleasurable living, was transformed into that of a strong and powerfully built knight-in-arms. Listen to what Boccaccio says in his version of the story: "Is there anything that love cannot accomplish? Here we see this lady, who was used to the finer things in life such as a soft bed and every possible comfort, choosing of her own free will to make herself as tough and rugged as any man, journeying over hill and dale, travelling by day and night, bedding down in deserts and forests often on the hard ground, in perpetual fear of the enemy and surrounded on all sides by wild beasts and serpents." Yet all this seemed agreeable to her as long as she could be at her husband's side to comfort and advise him, seeing to his every need.

'Later on, after having suffered many great hardships together, her husband was cruelly defeated by Pompey, a prince of the Roman army, and had to take flight. Though he was abandoned by all his men, his wife alone stayed with him, following him as he fled across mountains and valleys and through many dark and dangerous places. On the point of despair at having been deserted and forsaken by all his friends, the king was comforted by his faithful wife who gently encouraged him to hope for better days to come. Even when they were at their lowest ebb, she still made every effort to bring him good cheer and to lift his spirits by finding the right words to dispel his sadness and by inventing some amusing and distracting games for them to play together. By means of these things and her great kindness, she brought him such consolation that no matter how down-cast or dejected he was, or how much suffering he had to bear, she found a way to make him forget his unhappiness. He was often moved to say that he didn't feel like he was in exile but rather as if he were at home in his palace having a delightful time with his devoted wife.'

[...]

21. About Xanthippe, wife of the philosopher Socrates

The honourable lady Xanthippe was a very wise and virtuous woman who married the great philosopher Socrates. Though he was already very old and spent more time poring over his books than buying his wife little treats and presents, the good lady never stopped loving him. Indeed, she thought so highly of his extra-ordinary wisdom, as well as his great goodness and steadfastness, that she loved him very deeply and took enormous pride in him. When the brave and noble Xanthippe learnt that the Athenians had sentenced her husband to death for having attacked their practice of worshipping idols and for claiming that there was only one god whom they should honour and serve, she was unable to control her emotions. Rushing out into the street with her hair all undone and racked with sobbing, she fought her way into the palace where her husband was being held and found him surrounded by the treach-erous judges who were already handing him the cup of poison that would end his life. She came into the room just as Socrates had raised the cup to his lips and was about to drink the poison, whereupon she dashed it from his hands and spilt all the liquid on to the floor. Socrates chided her for this and tried to comfort her by telling her to have patience. Unable to do anything to prevent his death, she gave full vent to her sorrow, crying, "What a crime and a great loss it is to kill such a good man! What a sin and an injustice!" Socrates kept on trying to console her, explaining that it was better to be wrongfully put to death than to have deserved one's punishment. So he died, but throughout the rest of her life his loving wife never stopped grieving for him in her heart.'

[. . .]

25. Christine speaks to Lady Rectitude about those who claim that women cannot keep a secret. In her reply, Rectitude talks about Portia, Cato's daughter

'My lady, I am now totally convinced of what I have often seen for myself: many women of both the past and the present have clearly shown their husbands how much they love them and are devoted to them. That's why I'm so puzzled by a saying which is very common amongst men, including Master Jean de Meun in his *Romance of the Rose*, as well as other writers, that a man should avoid telling a woman anything which he wants kept secret because women are incapable of keeping their mouths shut.'

Rectitude replied, 'My dear friend, as you are aware, not all women are necessarily very wise and neither are all men. Therefore, if a man has any sense, he should judge for himself if his wife is trustworthy and well-meaning before he tells her anything in confidence, because it could have dangerous consequences. Any man who knows that his wife is dependable, careful and discreet can rest assured that there is no other creature in the world whom he can trust more implicitly nor on whom he can rely so completely.

'On the question of whether women are as indiscreet as some maintain, we also come back to the issue of wives who loved their husbands. The noble Brutus of Rome, who was married to Portia, certainly did not subscribe to this opinion. This fine lady, Portia, was the daughter of Cato the Younger, the nephew of Cato the Elder. Knowing how wise and virtuous she was, her husband did not hesitate to tell her that he and Cassius, another Roman nobleman, planned to kill Julius Caesar in the senate. However, foreseeing that this deed would have terrible repercussions, the sensible lady did her best to dissuade her husband from carrying out his plan. She was so disturbed by the thought of what he intended to do that she was unable to sleep at all that night. The next morning, as Brutus left the bedroom to go off and execute his plan, in a desperate attempt to stop him, Portia seized a barber's razorblade as if to clip her fingernails with it and dropped it on the floor. She then reached down to pick it up again and deliberately dug it deep into her hand. Horrified by the sight of her wound, her ladies screamed so loudly that Brutus turned back.

When he saw how she had cut herself, he scolded her and told her that it was a barber's job to use the razor, not hers. She replied that she hadn't acted as stupidly as he might think: she had done it on purpose in order to find out how to kill herself, should any harm come to him after he had carried out his plan. Still refusing to change his mind, Brutus left the house. Soon after, he and Cassius together killed Julius Caesar. They were sent into exile for what they had done and Brutus was subsequently murdered, even though he had already been banished from Rome. When his wife, Portia, learnt of his death, she was so distraught that she had no further desire to live. Since all the sharp instruments and knives had been taken away from her, because it was obvious what she intended to do, she went over to the fire and swallowed some live coals instead. The noble Portia thus killed herself by burning her insides, truly the strangest death that anyone has ever suffered.'

[. . .]

28. Proof against those who claim that only an idiot takes his wife's advice or puts his trust in her. Christine asks some questions to which Rectitude replies

'My lady, having heard your arguments and seen for myself how sensible and dependable women are, I'm amazed that some people claim that only a stupid idiot listens to his wife and trusts her advice.'

Rectitude replied, 'I pointed out to you earlier that not all women are wise. However, those men who do have responsible, trustworthy wives are fools if they refuse to put their faith in them. You can see this from what I've just told you: if Brutus had let Portia persuade him not to assassinate Julius Caesar, he himself would not have been killed and he could have avoided causing all the harm that was subsequently done. Whilst we're on this subject, I'll tell you about certain other men who suffered the consequences of not listening to their spouses. Afterwards, I'll go on to give you some examples where the husbands did well to take their wives' advice.

'If Julius Caesar, whom we've just mentioned, had trusted his sensible and intelligent wife, who had seen various signs foretelling her husband's assassination and had a terrible dream about it the night before, which made her do everything she could to try to stop him from going to the senate that day, he would not have gone and met his death.

'The same can be said of Pompey, who first married Julia, daughter of Julius Caesar, as I told you before, and then took as his second wife another noble lady, by the name of Cornelia. Going back to what we were talking about earlier, this lady loved her husband so dearly that she refused to leave him, no matter what misfortune befell him. Even when he was forced to escape by sea after having been defeated in battle by Julius Caesar, this good lady Cornelia went with him and faced every danger at his side. When Pompey arrived at the kingdom of Egypt, the treacherous King Ptolemy pretended that he was glad to receive him, sending his people ahead to welcome Pompey although in fact their mission was to kill him. These people told Pompey to get back on board ship and leave everybody else ashore so as to lighten the vessel of its load and thus manoeuvre it more easily into port. Pompey was happy to comply with their wishes but his loyal wife tried to dissuade him from separating himself from all his men by doing so. Seeing that he wasn't going to change his mind, she tried to jump back on to the ship with him because she suspected deep down that something was amiss. However, he wouldn't allow her to do so and had to have her held back by force. That was the point at which all this lady's sorrow began, a sorrow which was to haunt her all her life. No sooner had her husband sailed only a short way out than, having never taken her eyes off him for a second, she saw him being killed by the traitors on board. She was so distraught that she would have thrown herself into the sea if she hadn't been restrained.

'Likewise, the same sort of misfortune struck the worthy Hector of Troy. The night before he was killed, his wife Andromache had a most extraordinary dream which told her that if Hector went into battle the next day he would surely lose his life. Horrified by what she took to be not simply a nightmare but a true prophecy, this lady went down on her knees and begged her husband with hands joined together in supplication not to join the fighting that day, even bringing their two lovely children before him in her arms. However, he took no notice of her words, thinking that he would bring irreparable dishonour on himself if he allowed a woman's advice to stop him from going into combat. Neither was he moved by his mother's and father's entreaties after Andromache had asked them to intercede on her behalf. It thus all happened exactly as she had said and it would have been better for Hector if he had listened to her because he was killed by Achilles in battle.

'I could give you endless other examples of men who came to harm in various ways for not deigning to take their good wives' sensible advice. However, those who met a bad end because they dismissed what their wives had to say have only themselves to blame.'

[. . .]

31. About Judith, the noble widow

'Judith, the noble widow, saved the people of Israel from destruction at the time when Nebuchadnezzar II sent Holofernes to rule over the Jews, having conquered the land of Egypt. This Holofernes and his great army were besieging the Jews inside the city and had already inflicted so much damage on them that they could scarcely hold out much longer. He had cut off their water supply, and their stocks of food were almost exhausted. Despairing of being able to withstand much more, the Jews were on the point of being defeated by Holofernes and were in total dismay. They began to say their prayers, beseeching God to have mercy on His people and to prevent them from falling into the clutches of the enemy. God heard their prayers and, just as He would later save the human race by a woman, so He chose on this occasion to send a woman to their rescue.

'In the city lived a noble and valiant lady called Judith, who was a young and lovely woman of exemplary virtue and chastity. She took pity on the people in their distress and prayed to God day and night to save them. Inspired by God, in whom she had placed her trust, Judith hatched a daring plan. One night, commending herself to the Lord's care, she left the city accompanied only by one of her maid servants and headed for Holofernes's camp. When the soldiers who were on sentry duty saw in the moonlight how beautiful she was, they took her straight to Holofernes, who was delighted to receive such a dazzling woman. He made her sit down beside him and was soon entranced by her intelligence, proud bearing and beauty. The more he gazed at her, the more he burned with desire for her. She, who had other ideas, offered up a silent prayer to God to beg for His help in her endeavours, and managed to string Holofernes along with little promises until she could find the right moment. Three nights later, Holofernes threw a banquet for his barons and drank very heavily. Sated with food and drink, he couldn't wait any longer to sleep with the Hebrew woman so he sent for her to come to him, which she did. When he told her what he wanted, she was ready to do as he wished on condition that, for the sake of propriety, he made all his men leave his tent. He should then get into bed first, to be joined by Judith at midnight when everyone else was asleep. Holofernes accepted her terms. The good lady then began to pray, begging God to give her the necessary strength and courage in her trembling woman's heart to rid her people of this foul tyrant.

'When Judith thought that Holofernes would have fallen asleep, she and her maid servant crept up to the opening of his tent and stood listening. Hearing him sound asleep, the lady exclaimed, "Let's do it now, for God is with us!" She went inside and fearlessly grabbed hold of his sword that was hanging by the bed and drew it out of its scabbard. Using all her strength to lift the blade, she cut off Holofernes's head without making a sound. With the head wrapped in her skirts, she ran back to the city as fast as she could. Having returned to the gates without meeting any opposition, she called out, "Come and open up, for God is with us!" Once she was back inside, you can't imagine how overjoyed they all were at what she had done. In the morning, they impaled the head on a spike and stuck it on top of the city walls. They then threw on their armour and mounted a bold and swift attack on the enemy who were still sleeping, never once suspecting that this might happen. The enemy rushed to their leader's tent to wake him up and to get him out of bed as quickly as possible, but they were horrified to find him slain. The Jews took them all prisoner and killed every last one. Thus the people of Israel were delivered out of the hands of Holofernes by Judith, that valiant woman whose praises shall be sung for ever in Holy Scripture.'

[. . .]

33. About the Sabine women

'I could give you many examples of pagan women of antiquity who saved their countries, towns or cities. However, I'll limit myself to two important instances with which to prove my point.

'After the foundation of Rome by Romulus and Remus, Romulus filled the city with as many knights and soldiers as he could collect together after the numerous victories he had won. He was most anxious to obtain wives for these men in order that they would have heirs who would reign over the city in the years to come. However, he was unsure how to go about finding women for himself and his companions to marry, as the kings, princes and people in the surrounding country were reluctant to give them their daughters or to establish any links with them because they considered them to be too reckless, uncivilized and unreliable a race. For this reason, Romulus had to devise a cunning plan. He had it announced throughout the land that a tournament of jousting would take place and he invited all the kings, princes and citizens to come and bring their ladies and daughters to watch the entertainment provided by the foreign knights. On the day of the festivities, a vast crowd gathered on all sides, for a large number of ladies and maidens had come to watch the sport. Amongst them was the daughter of the Sabine king, a charming and beautiful girl, accompanied by all the other ladies and girls of her country whom she had brought along. The games took place outside the city walls, on a plain at the foot of a hill, with the ladies seated high up in rows. The knights outdid each other in their feats and exploits, for the sight of these lovely ladies inspired them to great deeds of bravery and daring. To keep my story brief, after they had been fighting for a while, Romulus decided that it was time to execute his plan and so took out a great ivory horn on which he gave a loud blast. At this sound, which was a signal for them to act, the knights stopped their jousting and ran towards the ladies. Romulus snatched the king's daughter, with whom he was already smitten, whilst the other knights each took the one they wanted. Forcing the ladies to get up on to their horses, the Romans galloped off towards the city and bolted the gates firmly behind them. Outside, the women's fathers and kinsmen let out great cries of grief, as did the ladies themselves who had been abducted, but their weeping was totally in vain. Romulus married his lady with great ceremony, and all the other knights did likewise.

'This event caused a terrible war to break out. As soon as he could, the Sabine king gathered a great army together to attack the Romans. However, it was not easy to defeat them as they were such experts in battle. The war had already lasted five years when, one day, the two sides prepared to meet in full strength on the battlefield and it was obvious that there was going to be an appalling massacre with enormous loss of life. The Romans had already left the city gates in huge numbers when the queen called all the ladies of Rome to meet together in a temple. This wise and beautiful young woman addressed them, saying: "Honourable Sabine ladies; sisters and companions, you all know only too well how we were abducted by our husbands and how this has caused a war between our fathers and kinsmen on the one side and our husbands on the other. There is no way that this deadly conflict can continue or even come to an end, without it being to our detriment, no matter who has the final victory. If we lose our husbands, whom we quite rightly adore now that we have borne them children, we shall be broken-hearted and devastated to see our babies deprived of their fathers. If, on the other hand, our husbands are victorious and our fathers and kinsmen are killed, we will surely deeply regret that all this conflict happened because of us. What is done is done and cannot now be undone. In my view, we need to find some way to bring this war to a peaceful end. If you decide to take my advice and follow my lead in what I'm going to do, I think that we'll be able to bring this about.' Hearing her words, the other ladies replied with one voice that they would do as she said and would obey her instructions.

'The queen therefore undid her hair and took off her shoes, as did all the other ladies. Those who had babies picked them up in their arms and carried them with them. In addition, there was a whole host of children, as well as pregnant women. The queen walked at the head of this touching procession and they all headed straight for the battlefield just as the two armies were lining up. They took up their position in between the opposing sets of troops, making it impossible for the knights to attack each other without first running into the women. The queen and all the other ladies fell to their knees and shouted out, "Dear fathers and kinsmen, beloved husbands: for God's sake, make peace! If not, we are prepared to die trampled underfoot by your horses." Seeing their wives and children in tears, the knights were astonished and dismayed: there was certainly no way that they would run at them. The women's fathers were similarly moved to compassion at the sight of their daughters in this terrible state. The two sides looked at each other and, out of pity for the women who were humbly begging them to desist, their hatred turned to proper filial love. Sabines and Romans alike were forced to throw down their weapons as they rushed to embrace each other and make peace. Romulus led his father-in-law, the king of the Sabines, into the city and received him and his whole army with great honour. Thus, thanks to the good sense and bravery of the queen and her ladies, the Romans and the Sabines were prevented from massacring each other.'

[. . .]

36. *Against those who claim that it is not good for women to be educated*

After hearing these words I, Christine, said, 'My lady, I can clearly see that much good has been brought into the world by women. Even if some wicked women have done evil things it still seems to me that this is far outweighed by all the good that other women have done and continue to do. This is particularly true of those who are wise and well educated in either the arts or the sciences, whom we mentioned before. That's why I'm all the more amazed at the opinion of some men who state that they are completely opposed to their daughters, wives or other female relatives engaging in study, for fear that their morals will be corrupted.'

Rectitude replied, 'This should prove to you that not all men's arguments are based on reason, and that these men in particular are wrong. There are absolutely no grounds for assuming that knowledge of moral disciplines, which actually inculcate virtue, would have a morally corrupting effect. Indeed, there's no doubt whatsoever that such forms of knowledge correct one's vices and improve one's morals. How could anyone possibly think that by studying good lessons and advice one will be any the worse for it? This view is completely unthinkable and untenable. I'm not saying that it's a good idea for men or women to study sorcery or any other type of forbidden science, since the Holy Church did not ban people from practising them for nothing. However, it's just that it's not true to say that women will be corrupted by knowing what's right and proper.

'Quintus Hortensius, who was a great rhetorician and a fine orator of Rome, did not subscribe to this opinion. He had a daughter named Hortensia, whom he loved dearly for her keen wits. He educated her himself, teaching her the science of rhetoric in which, states Boccaccio, she so excelled that she not only resembled her father in her intelligence, agile memory and excellent diction, but in fact surpassed him in her marvellous eloquence and command of oratory. On the subject of what we said before about all the benefits that women have brought, the good that this lady did is especially worthy of note. It was at the time when a triumvirate ruled over Rome that this Hortensia decided to take up the cause of women, thus performing a task which no man dared to do. As Rome was in great financial straits, it was proposed to levy certain charges on women and, in particular, to put a tax on their valuables. This Hortensia spoke so persuasively that she was listened to as attentively as if it had been her father speaking, and won her case.

'If we discuss more recent times, rather than going back to ancient history, Giovanni Andrea, the famous legist who taught at Bologna nearly sixty years ago, similarly opposed the view that women should not be educated. He gave his beloved daughter Novella, a fine and lovely girl, such a good education and detailed knowledge of law that, when he was busy with other tasks which prevented him from lecturing to his students, he could send his daughter in his place to read to them from his professorial chair. In order not to distract the audience by her beauty, Novella had a little curtain put up in front of her. Thus she lightened her father's load and relieved him of some of his duties. In his devotion to her, he chose to preserve her name for posterity by writing an important commentary on a legal text which he named *La Novella* in her honour.

'Therefore, it is not all men, especially not the most intelligent, who agree with the view that it is a bad idea to educate women. However, it's true that those who are not very clever come out with this opinion because they don't want women to know more than they do. Your own father, who was a great astrologer and philosopher, did not believe that knowledge of the sciences reduced a woman's worth. Indeed, as you know, it gave him great pleasure to see you take so readily to studying the arts. Rather, it was because your mother, as a woman, held the view that you should spend your time spinning like the other girls, that you did not receive a more advanced or detailed initiation into the sciences. But, as that proverb which we've already had occasion to quote says, "What is in our nature cannot be taken away." Despite your mother's opposition, you did manage to glean some grains of knowledge from your studies, thanks to your own natural inclination for learning. It's obvious to me that you do not esteem yourself any less for having this knowledge: in fact, you seem to treasure it, and quite rightly so.'

I, Christine, then replied, 'Without a doubt, what you're saying, my lady, is as true as the Lord's Prayer itself.'

37. Christine addresses Rectitude, who gives examples to contradict those who claim that few women are chaste, beginning with Susanna

'As far as I can see, my lady, all forms of goodness and virtue can be found in the female sex. So why is it that these men say that so few women are chaste? If this were true, all their other qualities would be worthless, because chastity is the supreme virtue in a woman. Yet, hearing what you've just said, the truth would seem to be very different from what they claim.'

Rectitude answered, 'The complete opposite is true, as I've told you before and as you yourself already know. I could keep telling you more on this subject until the end of time itself! The Holy Scripture mentions so many excellent and chaste ladies who preferred to die rather than lose their chastity, bodily integrity and good conscience. One such lady was the virtuous and lovely Susanna, wife of Joachim, who was a very rich and influential member of the Jewish race. As this honest lady was walking in her garden one day, she was approached by two old men, corrupt priests, who tried to tempt her into sin. Seeing that she completely rejected their advances and that their pleas were getting them nowhere, they threatened to denounce her in court for having been found with a young man. On hearing their threats, and knowing that the punishment for an adulterous woman was to be stoned, she exclaimed, "I am caught for all sides, for if I refuse to do what these men want, my body shall be put to death. But, if I give in to their demands, I shall be committing a sin in the eyes of the Creator. However, I would rather be innocent and suffer death than risk rousing God's anger by sinning." Susanna therefore screamed out loud and the other members of her household came running. To cut a long story short, the corrupt priests managed to convince the court with their false testimony and Susanna was sentenced to death. Yet God, who always looks after His own, opened the mouth of the prophet Daniel, who was just a small child in his mother's arms: when the boy saw Susanna being led to her punishment, followed by a great crowd of people who were all weeping, he cried out that the innocent woman had been wrongfully accused. She was taken back to the court where the corrupt priests were properly cross-examined and found guilty by their own confessions. The blameless Susanna was saved and it was they who were punished instead.'

[...]

44. In order to contradict those who claim that women want to be raped, here begins a series of examples, the first of which is Lucretia

I, Christine, then said, 'My lady, I fully believe what you say and I'm sure that there are many beautiful women who are upright, decent and fully able to protect themselves from the traps laid by seducers. It therefore angers and upsets me when men claim that women want to be raped and that, even though a woman may verbally rebuff a man, she won't in fact mind it if he does force himself upon her. I can scarcely believe that it could give women any pleasure to be treated in such a vile way.'

Rectitude replied, 'My dear friend, you can be sure that women who are chaste and lead a moral existence would find no pleasure in being raped. On the contrary, they think that it is the worst thing that could possibly happen to them. There are several examples, such as that of Lucretia, which prove that this is definitely the case. Lucretia, a high-born lady of Rome and, indeed, the most virtuous of all Roman women, was married to a nobleman called Tarquinius Collatinus. Unfortunately, Tarquin the Proud, son of King Tarquin, was deeply smitten with the great Lucretia. Having seen with his own eyes how supremely chaste she was, he didn't dare approach her directly. Despairing of being able to persuade her with bribes and entreaties, he plotted how to win her by trickery. He therefore pretended to be a close friend of her husband's, which meant that he was able to come and go as he pleased in her house. One day, when he knew that her husband was absent, he was welcomed most honourably by his noble hostess, as befitted a guest whom she took to be her husband's great friend. That night, Tarquin, who had other ideas, scared Lucretia out of her wits when he broke into her bedroom. In short, having made her numerous promises of gifts and presents if she would do what he wanted, he saw that pleading with her was getting him nowhere. He therefore pulled out his sword and threatened to kill her if she made a sound or refused to give herself to him. She told him to go ahead and kill her because she preferred to die rather than submit to his advances. When he realized that his threats were all in vain, Tarquin came up with another despicable ruse, declaring that he would let it be known publicly that he had found her with one of her servants. To cut a long story short, the thought that he would do such a thing so appalled her that she finally gave in to him.

'Yet Lucretia was unable to bear this awful offence with resignation. When morning came, she went to find her husband, father and close relatives, who were all the most prominent citizens of Rome. With great sobs and moans, she confessed to them the deed that had been perpetrated on her. As her husband and family were trying to comfort her in her terrible distress, she drew out a knife from under her gown, saying: "Though I can absolve myself of sin and prove myself innocent this way, I can't get rid of my suffering and pain: henceforth no woman need live in shame and dishonour because of what has been done to me." With these words, she plunged the knife deep into her breast and immediately fell down dead in front of her husband and his friends. Like madmen, they all rushed after Tarquin. The whole of Rome was incensed by what had happened: they deposed the king and would have killed his son if they had caught him. After that, Rome never had another king. Some say that because of the outrage done to Lucretia, a law was passed which sentenced to death any man who raped a woman, a law which is moral, fitting and just.'

[. . .]

47. *Proofs to refute the view that women are lacking in constancy: Christine asks questions, to which Rectitude replies with various examples of emperors who were unreliable and inconsistent*

'My lady, the women you've been talking about were certainly extremely steadfast, resolute and faithful. Could one say as much of even the strongest men who ever lived? Yet, of all the vices that men, and especially authors, accuse women of possessing, they are unanimous that the female sex is unstable and fickle, frivolous, flighty and weak-minded, as impressionable as children and completely lacking in resolution. Are men therefore so unwavering that it is utterly unheard of for them to vacillate, given that they criticize women for being so unreliable and changeable? If, in fact, they themselves are lacking in constancy, it's totally unacceptable for them to accuse others of having the same failing or to insist that others should possess a virtue which they themselves do not.'

Rectitude's reply was, 'My dear sweet friend, haven't you heard the common saying that fools are very quick to spot the mote in their neighbour's eye but slow to see the beam in their own? I'll show you just how unreasonable it is for men to criticize women for being inconstant and capricious. Their argument goes like this. First, they all assume that women are by nature weak. Then, having accused women of weakness, they presumably think themselves to be constant, or at least that women are not as constant as they are. Yet it's undeniable that they expect far greater constancy from women than they themselves can muster. Though they consider themselves to be so strong and to be made of such noble stuff, they're unable to stop themselves from falling prey to some awful vices and failings. Nor is this by any means always out of ignorance. Indeed, it's often down to deliberate bad intentions, because they're well aware that they're committing a sin. But they then excuse themselves, saying that to err is to be human. However, should a woman fall into error, usually thanks to a man's incessant scheming, lo and behold, they declare this to be due to women's innate weakness and inconstancy. Considering that they think women are so feeble, they should, rightly speaking, show greater tolerance of female frailty and not accuse women of dreadful sins that they consider to be only minor peccadilloes when they themselves are guilty of them. For there is no law, no written text, which says that they are allowed to sin more than women, or that their vices are any more excusable. None the less, they in fact give themselves such moral authority that, far from letting women get away with anything, they fall over themselves to impute to the female sex all manner of crimes and offences. Neither do they give women any credit for being strong and steadfast in the face of such awful criticisms. So, whatever the argument is, men have it both ways and always turn out to be in the right. You yourself have discussed this at length in your *Letter of the God of Love*.

'You asked me earlier whether men are so upright and worthy that they are justified in accusing others of inconstancy. I would say that if you examine human history from antiquity up to the present day, taking evidence from books and from both what you have seen with your own eyes in the past and what you can still see all around you today, and looking at men not just from the lower or uneducated classes but also from the upper classes, you can judge for yourself what perfection, strength and constancy they've displayed! This is the case with the vast majority of men, though there are some, thank heavens, who are wise, strong and steadfast.

'If you want me to give you examples of male inconstancy from the recent and distant past, since men persist in attacking women for this failing as if their own hearts were never subject to instability or change, just look at the behaviour of the most powerful princes and the most eminent men, in whom these are more dangerous faults than in others. Not to mention how many emperors are guilty of these things! I ask you, was the mind of a woman ever as weak, fearful, pathetic and frivolous as that of the Emperor Claudius? He was so unstable that whatever he ordered one minute, he reversed the next. It was impossible to take him at his word and he agreed with anything anybody said. In a fit of mad cruelty, he had his wife killed, and then, that night, he asked why she wasn't coming to bed! To those of his friends whom he had beheaded, he sent word that they should come and play with him! He was so lacking in courage that he lived in a constant state of fear and was unable to trust anyone. What can I tell you? Every kind of moral and mental debility was to be found in this atrocious emperor. But why am I just talking about this particular one? Was he the only ruler to sit on the imperial throne who was prey to such weakness? Was the Emperor Tiberius any better? Wasn't he more guilty of inconstancy, changeability and immorality than any woman has ever been?'

48. About Nero

'Whilst we're on the subject of emperors, what about Nero? It was glaringly obvious just how unstable and weak he was. Initially he was very laudable and made an effort to please everyone. Soon, however, his lechery, cruelty and greed knew no bounds. The better to indulge his vices, he would often arm himself at night and go off with his partners in crime to seek out places of depravity and corruption, amusing himself by running round town gratifying his obscene desires. As a pretext for committing his foul deeds, Nero would bump into people in the street and, if they said anything, he would attack them and kill them. He broke into taverns and brothels and raped women, on one occasion narrowly escaping death at the hands of a man whose wife he had raped. He organized lewd bathing parties and feasts that lasted all night. He would order first one thing and then another, as his capricious fancies took him. Nero indulged in all sorts of carnal pleasures, excesses and perversions, and there were no limits to his arrogance and extravagance. He loved those who were wicked and persecuted those who were virtuous. He was complicit in the murder of his father and he later had his own mother killed. When she was dead, he ordered her body to be opened up so that he could see where he had been conceived. Seeing her like that, Nero declared that she had once been a truly beautiful woman. He killed Octavia, his first wife, who was a fine lady, and took a second one, whom he loved at first but then had her murdered as well. He also ordered the death of Claudia, who had been the wife of his predecessor, since she refused to marry him. Nero similarly had his stepson killed when he was not yet seven years old purely because it was said of the boy that, when he was at play, his behaviour was obviously that of the son of an emperor.

'Nero's teacher Seneca, the noble philosopher, was also put to death by the emperor's orders, for he was unable to contain his shame at what was going on before his very eyes. Nero poisoned his prefect by pretending to give him a cure for his toothache. Likewise, he gave poisoned food and drink to the noblest of his princes and to the most venerable and illustrious of his barons, who exercised a great deal of power. Not only did he murder his aunt and seize all her wealth, but he also destroyed all the most notable families of Rome and drove them into exile, killing all their children in the process. He trained a ferocious Egyptian man to eat human flesh so that he could feed him living victims to devour. What can I tell you? It would be impossible to relate all his appalling crimes or the full extent of his foul wickedness. To cap it all, he set Rome on fire and let it burn for six whole days and nights. Many people died in this terrible catastrophe, whilst he stood singing on his tower, watching the inferno rage through the city and taking enormous delight in the beauty of the flames. At his dinner table, he had Saints Peter and Paul beheaded, as well as many other martyrs. For fourteen years he continued in this fashion until the Romans could finally take no more and rebelled against him. In his despair, he took his own life.'

[. . .]

53. After Rectitude has finished talking about women who were steadfast, Christine asks her why it is that all these worthy ladies of the past didn't refute the men and books who slander the female sex. Rectitude gives her answer

Such were the stories that Rectitude told me on this subject. Lack of space prevents me from going into detail on all the other examples she gave me, such as that of Leaena, a Greek woman, who refused to denounce two men who were friends of hers, preferring to bite off her own tongue in front of the judge in order to show him that no matter how much he tortured her he had no hope of extracting by force the information he wanted from her. Rectitude also told me about some other women who were so strong willed that they chose to die from drinking poison rather than fail to uphold truth and decency. I then turned to her and said, 'My lady, you've clearly demonstrated to me just how consistent and steadfast women are, in addition to all their other virtues. Surely there's no man of whom it could be said that he was their equal in this respect? I'm therefore amazed that so many worthy women, especially those who were learned and educated enough to write fine books in elegant style, could have allowed men to come out with their slanders all this time without contradicting them, when they knew only too well how false these men's accusations were.'

Rectitude replied, 'My dear Christine, this is an easy problem to solve. You should realize from what I've already told you that the virtuous ladies I've discussed with you were each involved in different types of activity and didn't all work towards the same end. This task of constructing the city was reserved for you, not them. These women's works alone were enough to make people of sound judgement and keen intelligence appreciate the female sex fully without their having to write anything else. As for the fact that the men who attacked and criticized women haven't yet been challenged, let me tell you that there's a time and a place for everything in the eternal scheme of things. Just think how long God allowed heresies against His holy law to prosper, which meant that they were very hard to stamp out and would still be around today if they hadn't been disputed and crushed. There are many things which flourish without hindrance until the time comes to take issue with them and refute them.'

I, Christine, came back to her again, saying: 'My lady, you're quite right. Yet I'm convinced that there will be plenty of dissenting voices raised against this very text. They'll say that, though some women of the past or the present might be virtuous, this isn't the case with all of them, or even the vast majority.'

Rectitude answered, 'It's just not true to say that the vast majority aren't virtuous. This is clearly proven by what I've said to you before: experience tells us that anyone can see for themselves, on any day of the week, how pious and full of charity and goodness women are. Not to mention the fact that it isn't women who are responsible for all the endless crimes and atrocities that are committed in the world. It's hardly surprising if not every single one of them is virtuous. In the whole of Nineveh, which was a very large city with a huge population, there wasn't one good man to be found anywhere when Jonah the prophet was sent by God to destroy it if the people didn't repent of their sins. Nor was there a single decent man living in the city of Sodom, as became clear when Lot left the place to be consumed by fire sent down from the heavens. What's more, you shouldn't forget that, though Jesus Christ's company only comprised twelve men, there was still one who was evil. To think that men dare to say that all women should be virtuous or that those who aren't should be stoned! I would ask them to take a good look at themselves and then let he who is without sin cast the first stone. Moreover, to what kind of behaviour should they themselves aspire? I tell you, the day that all men attain perfection, women will follow their example.'

54. Christine asks Rectitude if it's true what certain men have said about how few women are faithful in love, and Rectitude gives her reply

Going on to a different subject, I, Christine, spoke up once again and said, 'My lady, let's put such topics to one side and move on to something else. Departing a little from the kind of things we've been talking about up until now, I'd like to ask you a few questions. I hope you won't mind discussing these matters that I'd like to raise with you: although the subject itself relates to the laws of nature, it does somewhat overstep the bounds of rational behaviour.'

Rectitude's answer was, 'My friend, say what you like. The pupil who puts questions to his teacher in the spirit of enquiry shouldn't be reprimanded for touching on any subject whatsoever.'

'My lady, there's a kind of natural attraction at work on earth which draws men to women and women to men. This isn't a social law but an instinct of the flesh: stimulated by carnal desire, it makes the two sexes love each other in a wild and ardent way. Neither sex has any idea what it is that causes them to fall for each other like this, but they succumb in droves to this type of emotion, which is known as passionate love. Yet men often say that, despite all the protestations of fidelity that a woman in love may make, she not only flits from one lover to another but is also extraordinarily unfeeling, devious and false. They assert that this fickleness in women comes from their lack of moral character. Of all the various authors who have made such criticisms of women, Ovid is particularly virulent in his book, the *Art of Love*. Having attacked women for their lack of steadfastness in love, Ovid and all the others then go on to claim that they have written their books about the deceitful ways and sinfulness of women for the common good of all: their aim is to warn men about women's wiles and to teach them how to avoid them, just as if women were snakes hidden in the grass. So, my dear lady, please tell me what the truth of the matter is.'

Rectitude replied, 'My dear Christine, as for what they say about women being underhanded, I'm not sure what more I can tell you. You yourself have tackled this issue at length, when you refuted Ovid, along with all the others, in your *Letter of the God of Love* and the *Letters on the Romance of the Rose*. However, getting back to what you said about these men's claims to be writing for the common good, I'll prove to you that this is definitely not the case. Here's why: you can't define something as being for the common good of a city, country or any other community of people, if it doesn't contribute to the universal good of all. Women as well as men must derive equal benefit from it. Something which is done with the aim of privileging only one section of the population is called a private or an individual good, not a common good. Moreover, something which is done for the good of some but to the detriment of others is not simply a private or an individual good. In fact, it constitutes a type of injury done to one party in order to benefit the other: it thus only profits the second party at the expense of the first. Such writers don't speak to women in order to teach them to beware the traps laid for them by men, even though it's undeniable that men very often deceive women by their false appearances and cunning ruses. Besides, it's beyond doubt that women count as God's creatures and are human beings just as men are. They're not a different race or a strange breed, which might justify their being excluded from receiving moral teachings. I can thus only conclude that if these authors were really writing for the common good, they would warn women against the snares set by men as well as advising men to watch out for women.

'Let's leave these issues for now and go back to your earlier question. What I told you before about those examples of women whose devotion endured until the day they died obviously wasn't sufficient proof for you that, far from being as inconstant or as fickle in love as these writers maintain, the female sex is in fact extremely steadfast in matters of the heart [. . .]

62. Christine addresses Rectitude who, in her reply, refutes the view of those who claim that women use their charms to attract men

I, Christine, then said, 'My lady, you were quite right before when you said that passionate love was like a perilous sea. From what I've seen, women with any sense should do everything they can to avoid it, for they only come to great harm. Yet, those women who want to look lovely by dressing elegantly come in for a lot of criticism, because it's said that they only do so in order to attract attention from men.'

Rectitude answered, 'My dear Christine, it's not my business to try and find excuses for those women who are too fussy and obsessive about their appearance, for this is no small failing in a person. Wearing clothes that aren't fitting to one's station in life is particularly reprehensible. However, whilst I've no intention of condoning such a vice, neither do I want anyone to think that they have the right to lay more blame than is strictly necessary on those who make themselves beautiful in this way. I can assure you that not all women who do this are interested in seducing men. Some people, not just women but also men, have a legitimate taste and natural bent for taking pleasure in pretty things and expensive, elaborate clothes, as well as in cleanliness and fine array. If it is in their nature to behave like this, it's very difficult for them to resist, though it would be greatly to their credit if they did. Wasn't it written of Saint Bartholomew the Apostle, a man of high birth, that he spent his whole life draped in fringed robes of silk which were hemmed with precious stones, despite the fact that Our Lord preached poverty? Though such behaviour is usually rather pretentious and ostentatious, Saint Bartholomew can't be said to have committed any sin because it was in his nature to wear expensive clothes. Even so, some do say that it was for this reason that Our Lord was content for Bartholomew to be martyred by being flayed alive. My reason for telling you these things is to show you that it's wrong for any mortal creature to judge another's appearance; God alone has the right to judge us. I'll now give you some examples on this subject.'

[. . .]

64. Rectitude explains that some women are loved more for their virtue than others are for their attractiveness

'Even supposing that the reason women put such efforts into making themselves beautiful and seductive, elegant and alluring, *were* because they wanted to attract male attention, I'll prove to you that this does not necessarily mean that men who are decent and sensible are going to fall more quickly or more heavily for them. On the contrary, those men who value integrity are more readily attracted to women who are virtuous, honest and modest, and love them more deeply, even if they are less glamorous than flirts such as these. Now, some might retort that, since it's a bad thing to appeal to men in the first place, it would be better if those women who used their virtue and modesty to catch men's eyes didn't in fact possess such qualities at all. However, this argument is utterly worthless; one shouldn't refrain from cultivating things which are good and useful just because some idiots use them unwisely. Everybody should do their duty by acting well, no matter what happens.

'I'll now give you some examples which prove that many women have been loved for their upright and moral behaviour. Most notably, I could tell you about various saints of paradise whom men lusted after specifically for their purity. This is also what happened to Lucretia, whose rape I recounted to you earlier. It was because of her exemplary virtue, not simply her beauty, that Tarquin fell for her. One night, her husband was at supper in the company of some other knights, one of whom was this Tarquin who subsequently raped her. Each of them started to talk about his wife, claiming that his was the most virtuous of them all. In order to find out whose wife was the worthiest of this accolade, they rode off to call on each of their houses in turn. Those wives whom they found busy at some honest task or other were held in the greatest esteem. Of all the women, Lucretia was deemed to be the one who was spending her time in the most commendable way. Like the highly respectable and sober woman she was, Lucretia wore a plain gown as she sat with the other ladies of her household busily working wool and conversing on moral subjects. The king's son, Tarquin, who had accompanied Lucretia's husband, was so impressed by her integrity, her simple and laudable conduct, as well as her modest bearing, that he conceived a burning desire for her and began to hatch the wicked plan which he would later execute.'

[. . .]

66. Christine addresses Rectitude who, in her reply, refutes the opinion of those who claim that women are by nature mean

'I'm not sure what more to ask you, my lady, as all my questions have been answered. It seems to me that you've completely disproved the slanders which so many men have come out with against women. As far as I can see, it's even untrue what they so often say about avarice being the most prevalent of all the female vices.'

Rectitude replied, 'My dear friend, I can assure you that avarice is no more inherent in women than it is in men. Indeed, there would appear to be fewer avaricious women than men: as God knows and as you yourself can attest, the terrible evil that is so rampant in the world as a result of men's avarice is far greater than that which comes from women who possess this failing. However, as I pointed out to you before, the fool is all too ready to spot his neighbour's misdeed even though he is blind to his own great crimes.

'Just because women take pleasure in storing up cloth, thread, and all the other little items that are indispensable to a household, they earn themselves a reputation for being avaricious. Believe me, there are many, if not countless, women who, if they enjoyed great wealth, would not think twice about giving rewards and making generous gifts to those whom they thought would spend the money wisely. On the other hand, a woman who is poor is necessarily obliged to watch her pennies. In general, women are kept so short of money that they tend to hang on to the little they have because they know how hard it is to lay their hands on any more. Some people even go so far as to accuse women of being avaricious if they complain to their wayward husbands who are extravagant spendthrifts and beg them to be more careful with their money. Women like this know only too well how, thanks to the husband's foolish squandering, the whole household has to go without, and they and their poor children suffer as a result. This doesn't mean that such women are grasping or avaricious; on the contrary, it's a sign of their great prudence. Of course, I'm only referring to those wives who are discreet about admonishing their husbands. Otherwise this can cause great rows in marriage when the husband doesn't take too kindly to being criticized and ends up attacking his wife for something which is actually to her credit. As proof that this vice is not as common in women as some might say, just look at all the almsgiving that they eagerly perform. God knows how many prisoners, both in the past and still today, even those locked away in Saracen countries, have been comforted and helped out by women who were ready to give them money, not to mention how many poor people, impoverished gentlefolk and others they've also supported.'

I, Christine, then said, 'In fact, my lady, what you've just said reminds me of all the honourable ladies that I've seen making discreet displays of generosity, as far as their means allowed them. I know some of my female contemporaries take far greater delight in saying, "Here, take this" to someone who can put the money to good use than any miser ever did in grabbing some cash and hoarding it away in his coffers. I've no idea why men go around saying that women are avaricious. Although it's said that Alexander was famous for his generosity, I can tell you that I've seen little evidence for this!'

Rectitude burst out laughing and replied, 'My friend, the ladies of Rome were certainly not found wanting when the city was so heavily depleted by war that all the public funds to pay for troops were exhausted. The Romans were extremely hard pressed to find ways to raise money for the enormous army which they desperately needed. Out of their own great generosity, the ladies of Rome, including the widows, put all their jewellery and everything of value that they owned into a pile, which they then freely donated to the princes of the city. These ladies were very highly praised for their unselfish action. Their jewels were later returned to them, as was only right, for it was thanks to them that Rome's fortunes were restored.'

[. . .]

68. About the princesses and ladies of France

Once again I, Christine, interjected, 'My lady, now that you've reminded me of this woman of my own day and have started talking about the ladies of France, as well as those who have made their homes here, I would like you to tell me what you think of such women. Do you consider some of them to be worthy of inclusion in our city? Are they any less deserving of a place than foreign women?'

Rectitude replied, 'Certainly, Christine, I can assure you that there are many virtuous ladies among their number whom I'd be delighted to invite to become our citizens.

'First of all, we wouldn't refuse entry to the noble queen of France, Isabeau of Bavaria, who, by the grace of God, is now reigning over us. She has neither a shred of cruelty or greed in her body nor a single evil trait, for she is full of kindness and benevolence towards her subjects.

'No less worthy of praise is the young duchess of Berry, a wise, beautiful and gentle lady married to the Duke John, son of King John of France and brother of the late king, Charles the Wise. This honourable duchess conducts herself with such sobriety and discretion, even though she's still only a very young woman, that everybody commends her highly for her exemplary behaviour.

'What can I say about the duchess of Orleans, daughter of the late duke of Milan and wife of the Duke Louis, son of Charles the Wise, King of France? Could any lady be more prudent than she is? It's plain for all to see that she is not only steadfast and constant, but also very loving towards her husband and a fine example to her children. Moreover, she is astute in her affairs, fair-minded with everyone, sober in her bearing and endowed with every possible virtue.

'And what of the duchess of Burgundy, wife of the Duke John, son of Philip, who was himself son of the late King John of France? Isn't she also a fine lady, loyal to her husband, kind-hearted and well-disposed towards others, morally impeccable, and with no failing whatsoever?

'The countess of Clermont, daughter of the duke of Berry by his first wife, who is married to Count John of Clermont, son and heir of the duke of Bourbon, is everything that a noble princess should be in terms of her deep affection for her husband and her excellent upbringing in every respect, not to mention her beauty, wisdom and goodness. Her virtues shine all the more brightly thanks to her noble conduct and fine bearing.

'Amongst these ladies, there is one of whom you're particularly fond and to whom you're indebted as much for her own good qualities as for the kindness and affection you have received from her: this is the noble duchess of Holland and countess of Hainault, daughter of the late Duke Philip of Burgundy and sister of the present duke. Shouldn't this lady take her place amongst the ranks of the very finest ladies for her faithfulness, prudence and circumspection in her affairs, as well as her selflessness and extreme devotion to God? In a word, she is goodness itself.

'Doesn't the duchess of Bourbon also deserve to be commemorated for posterity alongside these other illustrious princesses, given that she is such an honourable lady, worthy of praise in every respect?

'What can I tell you? It would take me for ever to list the good qualities of all these ladies!

'The countess of Saint-Pol, daughter of the duke of Bar and first cousin to the king of France, also merits a place amongst these fine ladies, for she is kind and beautiful, noble and virtuous.

'Likewise, another lady to whom you're devoted, Anne, daughter of the late count of La Marche and sister of the present duke, who is married to Louis of Bavaria, brother of the queen of France, would not disgrace this company of splendid ladies whose praises should be sung to the skies. Both God and the whole world are witness to her excellent qualities.

'Despite what the slanderers may say, there's a positively infinite number of countesses, baronesses, ladies, maidens, bourgeoises and women of every estate who are honourable and distinguished. God be praised for keeping them all in virtue, and may He inspire those who are less than perfect to mend their ways. You must have no doubts about this, for I can assure you that it's the absolute truth, no matter what those who defame women out of envy might say to the contrary.'

I, Christine, then replied, 'My lady, it certainly gives me great pleasure to hear you say this.'

She then turned to me and said, 'My dear friend, it seems to me that I've now completed my task in the construction of the City of Ladies. I've not only built all the lovely palaces and splendid houses and mansions for you, but also filled them almost to overflowing with a vast number of wonderful ladies from all different ranks of society. My sister Justice will now come forward to put the finishing touches to the city, and I will say no more.'

69. *Christine addresses princesses and all other ladies*

'Most excellent, upstanding and worthy princesses of France and other countries, as well as all you ladies, maidens, and women of every estate, you who have ever in the past loved, or do presently love, or who will in the future love virtuous and moral conduct: raise your heads and rejoice in your new city. With God's help, it is now nearly complete, being resplendent with buildings and almost entirely filled with inhabitants. Thanks be to God for having led me through this difficult labour of learning in my desire to build an honourable and permanent place for you to dwell inside the walls of this city which will last for all eternity. I have come this far in the hope of being able to finish this task with the help of Lady Justice, who has promised me that she won't rest until she and I have done all we can to complete the city and shut its gates. So, pray for me, my worthy ladies!'

End of the Second Part of the Book of the City of Ladies.

Part III

1. The first chapter recounts how Justice brought the Queen of Heaven to live in the City of Ladies

Lady Justice came to me in all her glory and said, 'In my opinion, Christine, you have indeed done your very best to bring your task to fruition. With my sisters' help, you've made a fine job of building the City of Ladies. It's now time for me to add the finishing touches, as I promised you I would. I shall bring you a most noble queen, she who is blessed amongst all women, to dwell here with her fine company. She will govern and rule over the city and will fill it with the great host of ladies who belong to her court and household. I can see that the palaces and splendid mansions have now been decorated and made ready and that the streets are all covered with flowers to celebrate the arrival of both the queen and her retinue of most worthy and excellent ladies.

'So let all princesses, ladies and women of every rank come forth to receive, with honour and reverence, she who is not only their queen, but also reigns with supreme authority over all earthly powers, second only to her one begotten son whom she conceived of the Holy Spirit, and who is the son of God the Father. It's truly fitting that a gathering of the whole of womankind should beg this revered, noble and magnificent princess to deign to join their number and to live amongst them in their city here below. Nor will she despise them for their lowliness in comparison with her own greatness. There is no doubt that she, in her humility, which surpasses that of all other women, coupled with her goodness, which is greater than that even of the angels, will not refuse to live in the City of Ladies. She will reside in the highest palace of all, one that my sister Rectitude has already prepared for her, and which is entirely made up of glory and praise.

'Let every woman now come forward and say, with me, "We greet you, O Queen of Heaven, with an *Ave Maria*, the same greeting that the Angel of the Annunciation made to you and which gives you more pleasure than any other form of address. The whole of womankind now implores you to agree to live in their midst. Extend your grace and pity to them by acting as their protectress, shield and defender against all attacks from their enemies and the world at large. Let them drink deep from the fountain of virtues which flows from you and may they quench their thirst so fully that they learn to abhor all forms of vice and sin. Please come to us, O Celestial Queen, Temple of God, Cell and Cloister of the Holy Spirit, Dwelling-place of the Trinity, Joy of the Angels, Light and Guide of those who stray, and Hope of all True Believers. O my lady, who could dare even to think, let alone utter, the idea that women are vile, seeing how exalted you are! Even if the rest of womankind were evil, the light of your goodness shines out so brightly that it puts all wickedness into the shade. Since God decided to take a member of the female sex as His bride and to choose you, most excellent lady, because of your great worth, all men should not only desist from attacking women but should hold them in the highest esteem."'

The Virgin replied, 'Justice, my son's dearly beloved, I will gladly come to live amongst these women, who are my sisters and friends, and I will take my place at their side. This is because Reason, Rectitude, you Justice and even Nature, have all persuaded me to do so. Women serve, honour and praise me without end, thus I am now and ever shall be the head of the female sex. God Himself always wished this to be so and it was predestined and ordained by the Holy Trinity.'

Flanked by all the other women who fell to their knees and bowed their heads, Justice replied, 'My lady, may you be praised and honoured for all eternity. Save us, Our Lady, and intercede on our behalf with your son who refuses you nothing.'

[. . .]

3. About Saint Catherine

'The ladies whom we shall invite to form the company of the blessed Queen of Heaven, who is Empress and Princess of the City of Ladies, are blessed virgins and holy women. We shall thus prove that God loves the female sex by showing that He endowed women, just as He did men, with the strength and fortitude needed to suffer terrible martyrdoms in defence of His holy faith, despite the fact that these women were only tender, young creatures. The whole of womankind can benefit from hearing about the lives of ladies such as these, whose heads are crowned with glory, for the lessons which they impart are more edifying than any others. It is for this reason that they will be the most revered inhabitants of the city.

'The most eminent of these exemplary women is Saint Catherine, who was the daughter of King Costus of Alexandria. Though this worthy maiden was only eighteen years old when she inherited her father's lands, she conducted both her private life and her public affairs with great discernment. She was a Christian and had refused to marry, preferring to devote herself entirely to God. One day, the Emperor Maxentius came to Alexandria in order to perform an important sacrifice as part of a great ceremony in honour of the pagan gods. Catherine, who was at home in her palace, could hear the bellowing of the animals which were being prepared for the ritual slaughter as well as the loud clamour of music. She sent word to find out what was going on and was told that the emperor had already arrived at the temple to make the sacrifice. No sooner had she heard this than she went up to the emperor and began to speak to him most eloquently about the error of his ways. Being well versed in both theology and the sciences, Catherine used philosophical arguments to prove that there was only one God, the Creator of all things, and that He alone should be worshipped. When the Emperor Maxentius heard this beautiful and noble maiden speak with such extraordinary authority, he didn't know what to say but could only gaze deeply at her in amazement.

He sent for the wisest men that could be found in the whole of the land of Egypt, a country which was famous for the brilliance of its philosophers, fifty of whom were eventually brought to his court. However, once they realized why they had been summoned, they were extremely unhappy, saying that it was foolish of the emperor to have gone to all the trouble of bringing them from so far away simply to argue against a girl.

'To keep my tale brief, when the day of the debate arrived, the blessed Catherine blinded them with so many arguments that they were all convinced by what she said and were unable to answer her questions. The emperor was very angered by this and made all sorts of threats to them, but to no avail. By the grace of God, every one of them was won over by the virgin's holy words and became converted to Christianity. In his rage, the emperor sentenced all the philosophers to be burnt to death. The saintly virgin comforted them during their martyrdom, assuring them that they would be received into everlasting glory and praying to God to keep them strong in their faith. It was thus thanks to her that they took their place among the ranks of the blessed martyrs. God revealed His miraculous workings through them, for the fire destroyed neither their bodies nor their clothes: even after they had perished in the flames, not a single hair on their heads had been singed and their faces looked as though they were still alive. The tyrant Maxentius, who was inflamed with desire for the beautiful, holy Catherine, began to pay court to her in an attempt to persuade her to do his bidding. However, when he saw that he was getting nowhere with her, his pleas turned to threats and then to torture. He inflicted a cruel beating on her before throwing her into prison, with the express order that she was to be placed in solitary confinement for twelve days, at the end of which time he hoped to have starved her into submission. Yet the angels of the Lord went to her and gave her succour. When the twelve days were up, she was brought before the emperor once more. Seeing that she was even healthier and lovelier than ever, he was convinced that someone must have been visiting her in secret. He therefore ordered all the prison guards to be tortured. However, Catherine took pity on them and swore to Maxentius that the only comfort she had received came from God Himself. At a loss as to how to inflict an even crueller torture on her than before, the emperor took his prefect's advice and had wheels made which were fitted with razorblades. These wheels ground against each other in such a way that anything caught between them was torn to shreds. The emperor had Catherine stripped and forced her to lie between the wheels, yet she never once left off worshipping God with her hands clasped in prayer. The angels came down and smashed up the wheels, killing all the torturers standing nearby in the process.

'When the emperor's wife learnt about all the miracles that God was performing on Catherine's behalf, she converted to Christianity and criticized her husband for his conduct. She went to visit the holy virgin in her cell and begged her to pray to God for her sake. Because of this, the emperor had his wife tortured and her breasts cut off, whereupon the virgin said to her, "Most noble queen, don't be afraid of these tortures, for today you shall be received into neverending joy.'' The tyrant ordered his wife to be beheaded, at which sight huge numbers of his subjects converted. He asked Catherine to become his wife but when he realized that she was turning a deaf ear to all his pleas, he finally condemned her to be decapitated as well. In her prayers, she invoked the grace of God for all those who would remember her martyrdom and who would call out to her for help in their time of suffering. A voice came down from heaven saying that her prayer had been granted. As her martyrdom came to an end, milk, rather than blood, poured forth from her body. The angels took her saintly corpse and carried it to be buried on Mount Sinai, which was twenty days' journey away from Alexandria. God performed many miracles at her tomb, which lack of space prevents me from recounting: suffice to say that, from this tomb, flowed an oil which cured many illnesses. The Lord then punished the Emperor Maxentius in the most horrible ways.'

[. . .]

17. About Saint Afra, a repentant prostitute who turned to God

'Afra was a prostitute who converted to Christianity. She was brought before the judge, who said to her, "As if it weren't enough for you to sin with your body, you go and commit an error of faith by worshipping a foreign

god! Sacrifice to our gods and they will pardon you."
Afra replied, "I will sacrifice to my Lord, Jesus Christ,
who came down to earth for the sake of sinners. It says
in his Gospel that a female sinner washed his feet with
her tears and was forgiven. He didn't despise either
prostitutes or sinful publicans, but rather allowed them
to sit and eat with him." The judge retorted, "If you
don't agree to make a sacrifice, you'll never see any of
your clients again, nor will you receive any more presents
from them." She answered, "I will never again accept a
tainted gift. As for those that I did wrongfully receive,
I've asked poor people to take them away and to pray
for my soul." The judge sentenced Afra to be burnt to
death for having refused to worship the gods. As she was
being put into the fire, she glorified God, saying, "O
Lord Almighty, Jesus Christ, you who call all sinners to
repent, please accept my martyrdom in this hour of my
passion and deliver me from the everlasting fire by means
of this earthly fire that has been prepared for my mortal
body." As the flames leapt up around her, she cried out,
"Lord Jesus Christ, please receive me, a poor sinful
woman martyred in your holy name, you who made a
single sacrifice of yourself for the whole world. You were
a righteous man nailed to a cross for the sake of all those
who were immoral, a good man who died for the wicked,
a blessed man for the damned, a gentle man for the
cruel, an innocent and pure man for the corrupt. To you
I offer the sacrifice of my body, you who live and reign
with the Father and the Holy Ghost for ever and ever."
Thus the blessed Afra ended her days, on whose behalf
Our Lord later performed many miracles.'

d portcullises of our city. Although I
names of every single holy lady who
is still living, or is indeed yet to come,
mpossible for me to do so, they can all
their place in this City of Ladies, about
: "Gloriosa dicta sunt de te, civitas Dei."*
nding it over to you now that it is
ates are closed and locked, just as I said
nd may the peace of God remain with

the book: Christine addresses all
women

ladies, praise be to God: the construc-
finally at an end. All of you who love
fine reputation can now be lodged in
side its walls, not just women of the
of the present and the future, for this
nded and built to accommodate all
My dearest ladies, the human heart
vith joy when it sees that it has tri-
ular endeavour and has defeated its
moment on, my ladies, you have
ice – in a suitably devout and respect-
ing the completion of this new city.
lter you all, or rather those of you
yourselves to be worthy, but will

s are spoken of thee, O city of God.

18. Justice talks about several noble ladies who served the Apostles and other saints and gave them shelter

'My dear friend Christine, what more can I tell you on this subject? I could go on recounting an infinite number of such stories to you. Because you said before that you were so astonished at the amount of criticism that writers have heaped on women, I can assure you that no matter what you've read in the works of pagan authors, I think you'll find few negative comments on women in holy legends, in stories of Jesus Christ and his apostles, and even in lives of the saints. If you look at such texts, what you will find instead are countless instances of women who were endowed by God with extraordinary constancy and virtue. What great acts of kindness women have unstintingly and diligently performed for the servants of God! What exemplary charity and devotion they have shown them! So much hospitality and so many other kindnesses are surely not things to be taken lightly. Even if certain foolish men want to dismiss them as insignificant, it is undeniable that, according to our faith, such acts are the rungs on the ladders that lead to heaven.

'We can cite the example of Drusiana, a noble widow, who took Saint John the Evangelist into her home, where she served him and prepared his meals. Saint John returned from exile, much to the delight of the people of the city who came out to greet him, just as Drusiana's dead body was being lowered into the ground. She had died from grief at his lengthy absence. The neighbours said to him, "John, here lies Drusiana, the lady who was such a kind hostess to you and who died because you stayed away so long. She'll never serve you again." At this, Saint John exclaimed, "Rise up, Drusiana! Go home and get my food ready for me!", whereupon she was brought back from the dead.

'Likewise, we could mention the worthy Susanna, a noblewoman from the city of Limoges. She was the first person to give shelter to Saint Martial, who had been sent by Saint Peter to convert the French. This lady showed him every kindness.

'Likewise, the same can be said of Maximilla, that excellent lady who cut Saint Andrew down from the cross and buried him, thus putting her own life in danger.

'Likewise, the holy virgin Ephigenia was a devoted follower of Saint Matthew the Evangelist, whom she served. After his death, she built a church dedicated to him.

'Likewise, there was another fine lady whose pure love for Saint Paul the Apostle was so great that she went everywhere with him and served him most diligently.

'Likewise, at the time of the apostles, lived a noble queen by the name of Helen – not the mother of Constantine, but the queen of Adiabene – who went to Jerusalem. The city was desperately short of food because of a famine that was raging all around. When Helen learnt that Our Lord's saints, who had come to Jerusalem to preach to and convert the people, were dying of hunger, she bought enough food to keep them well supplied until the famine was over.

'Likewise, when they were taking out Saint Paul to be beheaded on Nero's orders, an honourable lady by

the name of
came up to h
her for the ve
handed it to
ing nearby n
up such a
blindfold hi
the blood-st
as a precio
that, for ha
do her a s
could tell y

'Basiliss
She was m
they mad
virginity.
this virgi
and maid
encourag
exemplar
Lord sp
deathbed

'My d
you. I c
differen
whose
God w
be eno
acquitt
high t
ladies,

as the gates an
haven't cited th
has ever lived, o
for it would be i
none the less tak
which we can say
I'm therefore ha
finished and the g
I would. Adieu, a
you always!'

19. The end of

'Most honourable
tion of our city is
virtue, glory and a
great splendour in
past but also those
city has been fou
deserving women.
is naturally filled v
umphed in a partic
enemies. From thi
every reason to rejo
able manner – at se
It will not only she
who have proved

*Glorious thing

also defend and protect you against your attackers and assailants, provided you look after it well. For you can see that it is made of virtuous material which shines so brightly that you can gaze at your reflections in it, especially the lofty turrets that were built in this final part of the book, as well as the passages which are relevant to you in the other two parts. My beloved ladies, I beg you not to abuse this new legacy like those arrogant fools who swell up with pride when they see themselves prosper and their wealth increase. Rather, you should follow the example of your queen, the noble Virgin. On hearing that she was to receive the supreme honour of becoming the mother of the Son of God, her humility grew all the greater as she offered herself up to the Lord as His handmaiden. Thus, my ladies, since it is true that the more virtuous someone is, the more this makes them meek and mild, this city should make you conduct yourselves in a moral fashion and encourage you to be meritorious and forbearing.

'As for you ladies who are married, don't despair at being so downtrodden by your husbands, for it's not necessarily the best thing in the world to be free. This is proven by what the angel of the Lord said to Esdras: "Those who used their free will fell into sin, turned their backs on God and corrupted the righteous; for this reason they were destroyed." Those wives whose husbands are loving and kind, good-natured and wise, should praise the Lord. This is no small boon but one of the greatest blessings in the world that any woman can receive. Such wives should serve their husbands with devotion, and should love and cherish them with a faithful heart, as is their duty, living in peace with them and praying to God to keep them safe and sound. Those wives whose husbands are neither good nor bad should none the less thank the Lord that they're not any worse. They should make every effort to moderate their husbands' unruly behaviour and to strive for a peaceable existence with them according to their social condition. Those wives with husbands who are wayward, sinful and cruel should do their best to tolerate them. They should try to overcome their husbands' wickedness and lead them back to a more reasonable and respectable path, if they possibly can. Even if their husbands are so steeped in sin that all their efforts come to nothing, these women's souls will at least have benefited greatly from having shown such patience. Moreover, everyone will praise them for it and will be on their side.

'So, my ladies, be humble and long-suffering and the grace of God will be magnified in you. You will be covered in glory and be granted the kingdom of heaven. It was Saint Gregory who said that patience is the key to paradise and the way of Jesus Christ. You should all resolve to rid yourselves henceforth of silly and irrational ideas, petty jealousies, stubbornness, contemptuous talk or scandalous behaviour, all of which are things that twist the mind and make a person unstable. Besides, such ways are extremely unhealthy and unseemly in a woman.

'As for you girls who are young virginal maidens, be pure and modest, timid and steadfast, for the wicked have set their snares to catch you. Keep your gaze directed downwards, say few words, and be cautious in everything you do. Arm yourselves with strength and virtue against the deceitful ways of seducers and avoid their company.

'As for you widowed ladies, be respectable in the way you dress, speak and hold yourselves. Be devout in your words and deeds, prudent in the way you run your affairs, and patient, strong and resilient in the face of suffering and aggravation, for you will have sore need of such qualities. Be unassuming in your temperament, speech and bearing, and be charitable in your actions.

'In short, all you women, whether of high, middle or low social rank, should be especially alert and on your guard against those who seek to attack your honour and your virtue. My ladies, see how these men assail you on all sides and accuse you of every vice imaginable. Prove them all wrong by showing how principled you are and refute the criticisms they make of you by behaving morally. Act in such a way that you can say, like the Psalmist, "The evil done by the wicked will fall on their own heads." Drive back these treacherous liars who use nothing but tricks and honeyed words to steal from you that which you should keep safe above all else: your chastity and your glorious good name. O my ladies, fly, fly from the passionate love with which they try to tempt you! For God's sake, fly from it! No good can come to you of it. Rather, you can be sure that though it may seem to be superficially attractive, it can only be to your harm in the end. This is always the case, so don't think otherwise. My dear ladies, remember how these men accuse you of being weak, flighty and easily led, and yet still use the most convoluted, outlandish and bizarre methods they can think of to trap you, just as one would a wild animal. Fly, fly from them, my ladies! Have nothing to do with such men beneath whose smiling looks a lethal venom is concealed, one which will poison you to death. Instead, my most honoured ladies, may it please you to pursue virtue and shun vice, thus increasing in number the inhabitants of our city. Let your hearts rejoice in doing good. I, your servant, commend myself to you. I beg the Lord to shine His grace upon me and to allow me to carry on devoting my life to His holy service here on earth. May He pardon my great faults and grant me everlasting joy when I die, and may He do likewise unto you. Amen.'

End of the Third and Final Part of the
Book of the City of Ladies.